HOW TO PRINT FABRIC

ZEENA SHAH

David and Charles

www.stitchcraftcreate.co.uk

FOREWORD BY KIRSTIE ALLSOPP

I first met Zeena on the set of my TV series *Kirstie's Vintage Home*, where I set up my own vintage workshop on London's Portobello road crammed with a wide range of skilled designer makers and plenty of handmade and homespun style. Zeena shared her printmaking expertise with me to create a beautiful lino printed blind for the series and her sewing know-how to upcycle vintage fabrics into adorable novelty pillows to accessorise your home with. It is a joy to see her now sharing her knowledge and printmaking skills in this beautiful book.

This book is full of brilliant and fun ideas with 20 exciting and original printmaking techniques that will have you addicted to printing fabrics with all manner of tools; from chopsticks and pencil ends to a lint roller. Zeena shows you how to print and sew some lovely projects using objects that you can find in your home and craft on your kitchen table top with very minimal and inexpensive equipment. You can even screen print with an embroidery hoop!

This book is the perfect companion for the beginner crafter, then advance your skills throughout the book building up to more complex makes. I couldn't think of a better way to spend an afternoon!

CONTENTS

INTRODUCTION

For as long as I can remember I have always loved to draw, and I was very much encouraged by my mum to endlessly craft and create things when I was younger. She would buy me and my sisters every 90s craft kit you can think of – basket weaving, cross stitching and pompom making, to name a few, and crafting has become more and more of an addiction ever since.

I first fell in love with print design when I was at art school, many moons ago now. I'd actually never thought in detail about the fabric printing process itself before this time, but from the moment I started experimenting with mark making, printing onto fabric and designing patterns, I knew I had found my thing!

Often in my printing classes or when I'm out running a stand at a lifestyle event I encounter lovely folk who really are terrified of printing – they are incredibly keen, but they're nervous to try it out on their own. So I want this book to bring printing onto fabric to everyone, especially to those at home – when I first left art school and set up my own silk screen printed homeware collection I was printing on the kitchen table and washing out my screens in the bathtub!

Here I'm going to demonstrate that you really don't need expensive or high-tech equipment to create a collection of beautiful print designs for fabric. I've therefore chosen printing techniques that you'll be able to master from your kitchen table, using a selection of minimal supplies that you're likely to find at the bottom of your recycling box. And for each printing technique I have also included a simple sewing project, so you can make your printed fabric into a beautiful item for your home or as a gift.

By the end of the book I hope to have inspired you to print and sew an assortment of lovely things for your home that you can proudly say you've made yourself when friends come over for dinner.

MARK MAKING

Mark making is a term that describes the process of using a tool to make a mark onto your printing surface, and this is one of the most exciting and experimental aspects of being a printmaker. There are no restrictions on what tools you can use – if you can insert an item into your fabric ink then press, roll or dab it onto your fabric to create an interesting mark, then you can and are printing with it!

Throughout this book I will guide you through a variety of techniques for mark making onto fabric. Relief printing is one technique, and describes the process of either carving into an object to create a varied printing surface, or creating a raised printing surface around an object as a block for printing. In this book we'll use anything from the elastic bands, string, cardboard and foam that you have around your home, to the more well-known soft rubber lino block material, to create original stamps for printmaking. Relief printing is a completely unique process, and it is perfect for the print design projects that follow, as well as for beginners who are getting to grips with the printing process itself.

I will also introduce you to stencilling as a process for mark making onto fabric. Different from the relief printing process, this method is a resist technique and uses stencils to block ink from the fabric itself. Ink is then applied directly across the fabric and the stencils are removed to reveal a print design. I'll show you how to create simple paper and tape stencils for stunning designs on your printed fabric.

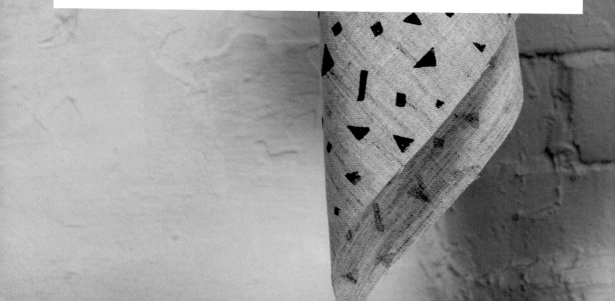

SCREEN PRINTING

Screen printing is a completely addictive process, and is what first hooked me into the world of textile design. In this book I'll guide you through different techniques for creating simple and more complex screen printed designs for fabric.

The term 'screen printing' itself describes the process of pushing ink through a woven mesh onto a printable surface. As the mesh pulls away from the surface it leaves behind an even layer of ink with a beautifully clear, crisp and unique finish that you wouldn't be able to achieve in any other way. The ink is pushed through the mesh using a rubber-ended tool known as a squeegee, and a stencil is used to block areas of the mesh to create a pattern.

All you need to practise this process is a screen, a squeegee and some screen printing ink. When choosing your screen I would recommend investing in a mesh screen with an aluminium frame, as it will last longer and it is far more lightweight than a traditional wooden framed screen. Squeegees are often the most expensive tool, but you can use a window cleaner's plastic squeegee to try out the process before you commit to buying one!

In this book I will take you through a range of screen printing techniques to create inexpensive stencils for simple one-off designs – using freezer paper, masking tape and an embroidery hoop. For more complex designs, I'll also introduce you to the permanent stencil making process (see Screen Printing with Photo Emulsion), which involves coating your screen mesh with a light-sensitive emulsion that will then be burned with your design.

By the end of this project you'll see it's not as complicated as you may have thought, and you'll have caught the printing bug!

INKS AND DYES

The choices for fabric printing inks are vast, and your own choice simply depends on what finish you want to achieve with your chosen printing technique.

I like to print with fabric screen printing inks that are slightly translucent to achieve a softer, more delicate finish. To create your own, mix acrylic paint and a fabric medium to thin the ink enough for printing – this is a method that provides endless colour options, but you can buy ready-mixed colours too.

These water-based screen printing inks work well on lighter coloured fabrics, but they aren't so good on darker fabrics where the colour beneath tends to show through. Primarily water-based and environmentally safe, fabric screen printing inks are easy to wash out of your printing equipment. They are also versatile enough to be used for both screen printing and for some of the mark making techniques in this book that don't require a heavier finish.

If you wish to create a more solid colour, a fabric block printing ink or a pre-mixed opaque fabric screen printing ink will provide you with the results you are looking for. These inks are much thicker, and will sit on the surface of the fabric rather than sinking into it like the water-based variety – this is great if you want to create a bold print design. They do require a little more care when you wash them out of your tools and your silk screen, but I find a little washing up liquid always helps.

Fabric dyes are often neglected but actually create a lovely finish for mark making techniques. They can be mixed with water to your desired colour then painted directly onto fabric rather than solely being used for dipping tools into, providing a way to create a beautiful watercolour print effect with the simplest of tools.

Rather than always using an ink to add colour to your fabric, you can also experiment with bleach as a means of stripping the colour from your fabric to create a print. You do need to choose a darker fabric for this method of mark making, but the beauty is in the reveal when the bleach has worked its magic.

For each project in this book I have suggested the best ink to use, and as you work through you'll begin to get a feel for the different types of inks and why they work well for a particular printing technique. Much of the time it is simply down to trial and error in accomplishing the best results – in this case practise really does make perfect!

FIXING, WASHING AND HANDLING

Once you have spent all that time printing your fabric, it is important to fix the ink correctly in order to maintain the colourfastness of the print over time.

Heat setting your print is an easy way to do this – cover the print with a cloth to prevent any colour transferring, then iron the printed fabric for several minutes, using a medium to hot setting. In addition, your individual fabric printing inks should include instructions for fixing the colour to the fabric with that specific product, so do read these carefully.

When your fabric is fixed, you'll be able to wash it in a cool handwash or at 30°C in your washing machine without any fading.

FABRICS

I am so easily distracted when I head off into town for a spot of fabric shopping – I really am spoilt for choice here in London with so many colours, textures and patterns available. However, you do need to choose your fabrics wisely when it comes to printing.

There are some incredible man-made fabrics around, but I would recommend you avoid them, using only natural fabrics instead. This is because man-made fabrics generally have unnaturally smooth or shiny finishes or coatings, so you may have trouble getting your ink to fix to them properly or you may not be able to print sharply enough onto them.

My favourite fabrics to print on are natural cottons, canvases, calicos, linens and wool felts, which are readily available in varying weights and textures. The smoother the fabric and the closer the weave, the clearer and sharper your print will be. However, it's fun to experiment with natural fabrics that are a bit more textured, as their different qualities can lend themselves well to a particular printing technique.

For example, a lovely heavyweight linen is great for making a sturdy pocket, but has a rough texture for printing – this means you need to adjust your design or choice of print for the particular fabric type. In this instance I would print a simple silhouette with minimal detail to use the heavyweight linen to its best advantage. A delicate design would not print well on a heavily textured fabric, so for this kind of design I would choose a fine linen or cotton.

Plan your projects before you begin working on them and make sure your fabric will fit the purpose – soft brushed cotton is wonderful for making a baby bib, but it won't be sturdy enough as the fabric for a laundry bag. It is also always good practice to wash your fabrics before you begin printing on them, as this will remove any residue from the factory or elsewhere that could affect your printing ink. When you are printing, it's best not to leave anything to chance, and always to be prepared.

I tend to choose lightly coloured or lightly patterned fabrics to print on so I can achieve the colours I want without disappointment. If you do choose to print with a coloured or darker fabric, just remember that your ink may print slightly differently to the colour in the pot – you can try opaque inks to achieve a bolder colour.

It is always a good idea to sample your printing techniques on a selection of fabrics if you're struggling to make up your mind. Most fabric stores will let you take a sample away with you before you commit to buying a larger quantity.

My best advice would be to spend as much time as you can experimenting with your designs to really appreciate the differences between fabrics and the beauty of fabric printing. You will learn by doing so, and this is where the magic happens!

UNDERSTANDING PRINT DESIGN

Creating your own print design for the first time can be a daunting task, so here I have listed some key design principles to guide you when you're thinking up design ideas and preparing your motifs. Once you get to grips with these basic rules and processes, you'll be able to experiment with layouts, building up to create more complex designs.

POSITIVE AND NEGATIVE SPACE
Throughout this book I will refer to the space within and around your design motif – the positive space is the motif itself, while the negative space is the background area of the motif. These terms are used in the relief printing techniques where you will need to cut away areas for printing. If you are clear on the difference between positive and negative space, it will be much easier to understand which areas you need to keep and which areas you need to remove to create your print designs.

SINGLE MOTIF All print designs begin with a single motif. You can use it as a stand-alone design, which is also known as a placement print. Think about the placement of the single motif on your fabric, as it doesn't have to fill the entire space, but could just fill a border or a corner instead.

SPOT REPEAT This is the simplest type of repeat pattern. Your motif repeats from top to bottom and right to left with even spacing. Simply rotate or add another variation of the motif to bring movement to this type of pattern design.

HALF-DROP REPEAT Each motif drops down halfway across each vertical of the design. Vary this by trying a quarter or three-quarter drop to create multiple pattern designs.

BRICK REPEAT Imagine you are laying bricks with your design motif. This pattern design shifts on the horizontal to build its repeat.

MIRROR REPEAT This is an easy way to add a bit of variation to a single image or motif. Simply mirror then alternate your motif across the pattern design.

RANDOM REPEAT Working within a square, fill the area with motifs placed randomly to create a more haphazard pattern design and loose style of repeat.

CUT-THROUGH REPEAT To create a seamless repeat you will need to follow the cut-through process. Start with a motif (A) then cut it through the centre vertically, flipping each side to the opposite edges to create a gap in the centre (B). Fill the central space with more of your pattern, avoiding the edges (C). Now cut through the motif centre again, but this time horizontally (D). You will have completely distorted your original image, but you should have a space in the centre. Fill the centre with another motif or part of your design (E). You will now have a completed repeat block pattern. Duplicate this across your fabric, lining up the edges as you go, to create your repeat pattern design (F).

Positive and Negative Space

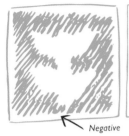

Negative

Positive

Single Motif

Spot Repeat

Half-drop Repeat

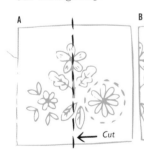

Brick Repeat

Mirror Repeat

Random Repeat

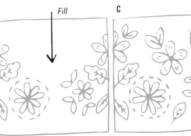

Cut-through Repeat

A

Cut

B

Fill

C

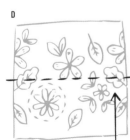

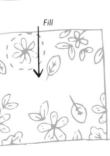

D

Cut

E

Fill

F

THE PROJECTS

In this section you will find 20 different techniques for printing onto fabric – then each one is followed by a simple sewing project. I want you to be able to create something immediately (to show off!) using your newly acquired printing skills, so refer to the sewing project for exact fabric dimensions if you want to use your printed fabric to make this item. However, you can also mix and match the printing techniques you learn throughout this book to any of the sewing projects.

For those of you who are new to printing and sewing, don't worry. I've given each printing technique and sewing project a difficulty rating – just use the number of hearts shown on each project as a guide (see below). I would suggest that you start with the simple projects that have just one heart then build up to those with three as you advance.

Although you will need a sewing machine for many of the projects, I have indicated within the project steps where you can complete the sewing by hand. I have also added some 'no sew' projects (see Hexagon Trivet, Tea Towel and Forest Drum Lampshade) if you want to craft something beautiful but don't have much time. Enjoy!

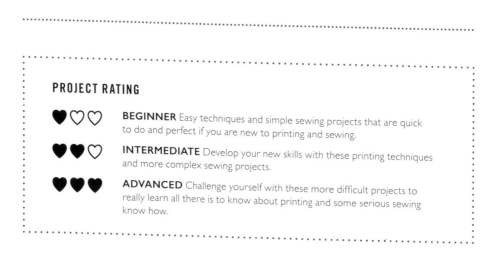

PROJECT RATING

♥♡♡ **BEGINNER** Easy techniques and simple sewing projects that are quick to do and perfect if you are new to printing and sewing.

♥♥♡ **INTERMEDIATE** Develop your new skills with these printing techniques and more complex sewing projects.

♥♥♥ **ADVANCED** Challenge yourself with these more difficult projects to really learn all there is to know about printing and some serious sewing know how.

ELASTIC BAND PRINTING

If you are anything like me you'll have hundreds of elastic bands lying around the house. I can't bear to throw them away, so I have a brilliant way to re-use them for printing fabric. Simply twist your bands around a cardboard box or any solid object then stamp away with a fabric inkpad to create a unique pattern design.

01 Wrap the elastic bands around a matchbox or similar item. You can overlap them, but try to keep them as flat as possible for a better print.

02 Test your pattern on a piece of scrap paper by pressing the inkpad firmly onto the elastic band stamp then pressing the stamp face down onto the paper. Apply pressure evenly then lift up to reveal your print.

03 Wipe the ink from your stamp with a baby wipe then make any necessary adjustments to the positions of the elastic bands. Repeat this process to test the stamp on scrap paper again until you are happy with the result.

04 Lay out your fabric ready for printing then use your inkpads and elastic band stamp to print a repeat pattern design, working from the top of the fabric to the bottom. Use a pencil or trick marker and a ruler to mark out where your prints will go.

05 Build up your design using different coloured inkpads, making sure you remove each colour with a baby wipe before you apply a new one. Continue this way until you have covered your fabric with print!

YOU WILL NEED

- Fabric, medium weight
- Fabric inkpads for stamps
- Elastic bands, an assortment
- Matchbox or similar cardboard item
- Pencil or trick marker
- Ruler
- Baby wipes
- Scrap paper

Tip: Inkpads are so versatile you can achieve a surprisingly strong colour with them. You can also try mixing two colours together to create an ombré print.

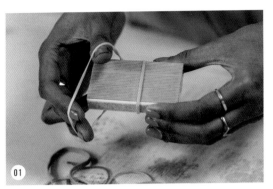

01

02

03

04

05

TABLET SLEEVE

Stitch yourself a practical and pretty sleeve for your tablet. With a felt lining this cover is both functional and sturdy, and it will protect your tablet when you're out and about. Add a contrasting coloured elastic fastening for the perfect finishing touch.

01 Print your fabric using the Elastic Band Printing technique. Dry and fix as the manufacturers of your ink products recommend.

02 With your fabric facing the wrong side up, turn the edges in 1.5cm (⅝in) all the way around and press into place (A). Make the corners as neat and flat as you can.

03 With the wrong side still facing up, place one piece of felt directly on top – it should fit exactly – and pin it into place (B). Then sew 3mm (⅛in) in from the edge around all four sides to create the front piece of your tablet sleeve.

04 Next stitch the elastic together, overlapping the ends to loosely fit around the tablet sleeve cover (C). Use a sewing machine to stitch, reversing back and forwards a few times to secure the stitching.

05 Attach the elastic to the back felt piece of your tablet sleeve by pinning it into place approximately 2cm (¾in) in from the right-hand edge then sew across the elastic at 7cm (2¾in) and 14cm (5½in) intervals, securing at two points for extra strength (D).

06 Pull the elastic out of the way and, with the right sides facing out, pin the front and back pieces of your sleeve together. Stitch 3mm (⅛in) in from the edge around all three sides, leaving the top open and moving the elastic out of the way as you sew – reverse at the start and finish to secure the stitching.

07 Trim any excess threads then slip in your tablet.

YOU WILL NEED

- Printed fabric, 24.5 x 18cm ((9½x 7in)
- Two pieces of felt fabric, 21.5 x 15cm, (8¼x 6in)
- Elastic, 50cm (20in) in length
- Sewing machine and matching thread
- Scissors
- Tape measure
- Pins
- Iron

Tip: Really personalize your tablet cover by attaching the elastic either to the right, left or in the centre of the cover. Make it your own!

(A) 1.5cm (⅝in)

(B) Felt

Printed fabric

(C) Stitch

(D) 7cm (2.7 in) 14cm (5½in)

2cm (0.7in) Back

PENCIL END PRINTING

Gaining inspiration for print designs by using everyday objects is something I love to experiment with, plus this is a great idea if drawing isn't your strong point. All you need is something as simple as the end of a pencil to create a unique repeat pattern on your fabric.

01 With a pencil, trace around the Hexagon template (see Templates) directly onto your felt. Then carefully cut out the shape, using sharp scissors or a scalpel and cutting mat.

02 Prepare your fabric ink ready for printing. Then squeeze a pea size amount of ink into a dish and use a paintbrush to spread it out into a smooth, thin layer.

03 Dip the rubber end of a pencil directly into the ink then press it firmly onto a test piece of felt, lifting it off to reveal your print. Experiment with the marks you can make – overlap them, vary the spacing, and alternate the direction to create a series of patterns you can choose from for your final design.

04 Use a ruler and trick marker to mark a guideline for printing onto the felt hexagon, making a point every 2 to 3cm (¾ to 1⅛in) that is evenly spaced both vertically and horizontally to create a consistent repeat pattern. The trick marker will fade within 24 hours so it won't affect the final print.

05 Print onto the hexagon piece of felt following the guidelines, starting at the top and working your way down to the bottom – this is to keep your hands away from the wet ink so you avoid smudging the print. The beauty of this printing technique is that each mark is completely different from the next, which is something that can only be achieved by hand.

YOU WILL NEED

- Felt fabric, 3mm (⅛in) thick
- Opaque fabric block printing ink
- Dish
- Paintbrush
- Pencil with a rubber end
- Trick marker
- Scissors, or scalpel and cutting mat
- Ruler

Tip: Vary the pressure on your pencil while printing to achieve a mottled or more solid print mark. I love the inconsistencies of printing by hand.

HEXAGON TRIVET

A trivet is a useful and decorative addition to any kitchen table for all your hot pots to rest on. This one is a brilliant no-sew project that you can create simply by using your new printing skills and a piece of felt.

01 Trace your Hexagon template then use it to cut out a felt trivet shape. Use the Pencil End Printing technique to print the fabric with your chosen design. If you are feeling adventurous, experiment with more than one colour, try creating geometric patterns with the end of your pencil, or a striped pattern.

02 Dry your print with a hairdryer and fix the felt following the instructions on your ink product. Once dry, I cover the felt with a tea towel or scrap piece of fabric and iron on a medium heat to set the ink into the fabric.

03 Once fixed, your trivet it is now ready to use.

YOU WILL NEED

- Printed felt fabric hexagon
- Hairdryer
- Iron

Tip: You can use the same technique to create a matching set of coasters and placemats by either cutting out similar shapes or drawing around a mug for a circular shape.

NO-SEW
PROJECT

FOAM STAMP PRINTING

Print foam is a really versatile material and yes, it's the stuff that comes with your frozen pizza! You can use it as an alternative to a lino block as it's so sturdy, and it produces a lovely finish when used for printing. You can also cut it up and mount it at the ends of old corks to create an inexpensive set of practical recycled stamps. This is a fantastic project for beginners.

01 Using the tracing paper and a soft leaded pencil, transfer trace the Baby Bib templates (see Templates) onto your print foam block.

02 Cut out your shapes from the foam block carefully, working with a scalpel and cutting mat to create a nice, clean finish to the stamp shapes for printing.

03 With a little all-purpose glue, mount each foam shape onto a cork bottle top. Press firmly to make sure each is securely attached then leave to dry before using.

04 Prepare your inks for printing by rolling out a thin layer into your ink tray with a roller or brayer. Make sure it is evenly spread, as the finer the layer of ink, the sharper the print and the better the finish will be.

05 It is always a good idea to test your stamp on a piece of scrap fabric before printing your final design. Dip the stamp into the ink tray and press it firmly onto the scrap fabric – the firmer the pressure, the more even the print.

06 When you are happy with your stamp, work from the top edge of the fabric to the bottom to print your final design. Dry one colour before adding the next to avoid smudging your prints then continue to build up your design.

YOU WILL NEED

- Plain fabric, soft brushed cotton or similar
- Fabric block printing inks
- Ink tray
- Roller or brayer
- Print foam block
- Cork bottle tops
- Soft leaded pencil
- Scalpel and cutting mat
- All-purpose glue
- Tracing paper
- Scrap fabric

Tip: Create more complex multi-coloured prints by using a different stamp for each different colour layer, working with one stamp at a time to build up your design.

01

02

04

03

05

06

BABY DRIBBLE BIB

Use your print foam stamps to make this adorable and functional baby dribble bib, which will make a great gift for new-born babies too. Simply tie the ends together and slip it over your little one's head.

01 Fold an A4 (letter) sheet of paper diagonally, from the top right edge to the bottom left, then cut along this line with scissors. Use one half for your dribble bib pattern, marking in a fold line along the shortest edge (A).

02 Fold your fabric in half and pin the paper pattern to it, aligning the fold line on the pattern with the fold in the fabric. Cut twice so you have two identical pieces of fabric, one for the front and one for the back of the bib.

03 Print the front piece of your fabric using the Baby Bib templates and the Foam Stamp Printing technique. Dry and fix following the instructions specified on your printing ink.

04 With the right sides facing, pin the pieces of fabric together, inserting the pins at right angles. Leave a 2 to 3cm (¾ to 1⅛in) gap along one edge for turning later (B).

05 Sew around the edges of your fabric pieces with your sewing machine or by hand with a close running stitch or back stitch (see Sewing Techniques), leaving a 1cm (½in) seam allowance. Trim down the edges so they are even, as well as any excess threads, then use scissors to square off the corners (C).

06 Turn the bib the right side out then press using an iron. Tidily tuck any excess seam back inside the gap and press again. Pin into place then top stitch with your sewing machine or by hand (see Sewing Techniques) as close to the edge as you can all the way around, using matching or contrasting coloured thread, to complete the bib!

YOU WILL NEED

- Printed fabric (see Steps 01 and 02)
- Sewing machine and matching thread
- Hand-sewing needle
- Scissors
- Pins
- Iron
- Sheet of paper, A4 (letter) size

Tip: Make your bib reversible by printing a different design on each side of your fabric, varying the colours and using contrasting thread to make it truly unique.

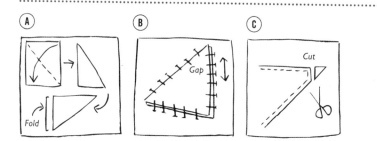

BLEACH MARK PRINTING

In this project I'm going to show you how to use some basic household bleach to create a pretty printed fabric. Rather than printing with colour, this time we will be removing the colour to achieve our design – all you need is some dark coloured fabric and wooden tools to print with. I've saved the free chopsticks from restaurants especially for this technique, but you can use anything, from the end of a pencil to cocktail (orange) or lollipop sticks.

01 Cut a scrap piece of fabric into small sections ready for test printing. Lay these out on some scrap paper or a table protector.

02 Pour a little bleach into a pot then dip your chopstick or other chosen wooden tool directly into it. Dunk it in the bleach evenly and make sure it doesn't drip on the fabric and create unwanted marks. Bleach can burn your skin so handle it carefully.

03 Press the bleach-coated wooden tool down firmly onto a piece of your scrap fabric, lift it up then repeat this process to continue your mark making. The bleach will take a few minutes to work its magic then it will remove the colour to reveal a lovely uneven mark that resembles the shape of your chosen tool.

04 Experiment with the different tools you have chosen on your scrap fabric pieces. Mix up the shapes and play with layout ideas to create different repeat patterns.

05 Cut out your fabric pieces using the Pyramid Doorstop templates (see Templates) then mark out your chosen design onto them with some chalk and a ruler so you know where to place your marks. Print with your final design by following these guidelines then leave to dry.

YOU WILL NEED

- Dark coloured natural fabric, medium to heavyweight
- Bleach
- Wooden tools for printing, chopsticks, lollipop sticks, cocktail (orange) sticks, pencil
- White chalk
- Scissors
- Ruler
- Scrap fabric
- Scrap paper or a table protector

Tip: Experiment with this technique to try printing through a piece of lace to create different patterns.

01

02

03

04

05

PYRAMID DOORSTOP

This handy doorstop is a quick and easy sewing project, plus it's a great way to inject a little pattern into an otherwise boring home accessory. Use triangular pieces of fabric to create your pyramid shape, add a hanging loop, stitch and fill. Then you're ready to prop open your door with it!

01 Cut out your fabric pieces using the Pyramid Doorstop templates and print using the Bleach Mark Printing technique. Dry and press ready for sewing.

02 With the right sides facing, pin then sew two triangles together with a 1cm (½in) seam allowance, reversing at the top and bottom of your seam to secure (A). Press and finish the seams (see Sewing Techniques) then repeat the process for the other two triangles.

03 Place both double triangle pieces together, right sides facing, then pin into place. Slip the felt loop handle inside the top edge with about 1cm (½in) poking outwards, pin into place then sew the remaining two edges together to create a hollow diamond shape (B).

04 Next attach the base piece of fabric by lining it up along each triangle edge with the right sides facing and pinning it into place (C). Sew it carefully, leaving a 10cm (4in) gap along one edge for adding the filling later.

05 Turn the pyramid the right side out, tucking the raw edges inside, and press then fill with your chosen filling. As you near the top, give the doorstop a shake to remove any air pockets then continue to fill right up.

06 Pin the open edge closed and use a needle and thread to slip stitch (see Sewing Techniques) this closed, hiding the raw edges inside.

YOU WILL NEED

- Four triangles of printed fabric, base 16cm (6in), height 16cm (6¼in)
- Square of plain felt fabric for the base, 16 × 16cm (6¼ × 6¼in)
- Felt for loop handle, 15 × 2cm (6 × ¾in)
- Sewing machine and matching thread
- Hand-sewing needle
- Chalk
- Scissors
- Ruler
- Pins
- Filling, rice, pulses or sand in a plastic bag
- Iron

Tip: Use a more sturdy fabric such as dark coloured felt for the base to hide any dirty marks from the floor.

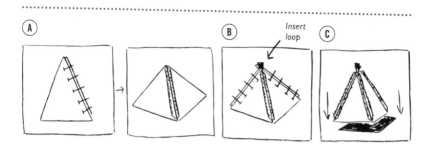

FALLEN LEAF PRINTING

I draw a lot of inspiration for my print design collections from nature – the colours, shapes and changing seasons have a real impact on my work. Collecting natural found objects is a wonderfully fun way to spend an hour outdoors then you can use your collection to create a striking printed fabric design.

01 Press the fabric so it is completely flat with no visible creases that could affect your print. Then use some tape to secure it in place so it doesn't move during the printing process.

02 Gather your collection of leaves, selecting your favourite shapes and a mixture of sizes for variation. Arrange these all over your piece of fabric so they look like they have just fallen from a tree. Alter their direction and vary their sizes to build up an interesting print design.

03 Spread some fabric ink in your ink tray using a paintbrush then carefully dab ink onto the underside of one leaf with a sponge. Start finely then build up the ink so the leaf is evenly coated.

04 Carefully flip the leaf onto the fabric, ink side down. Hold it in place with one hand and gently apply pressure using a roller with the other hand to ensure an even print.

05 Lift up the leaf to reveal your print! You'll be able to see it has picked up all the beautiful details of the leaves. Experiment with the amount of ink you put on each leaf to vary your print design.

06 Repeat this process with the other leaf shapes you have selected, experimenting with the amount of ink you put on each leaf, as well as a different colour or two to vary the effect. This will create a lovely all-over multi-coloured print design ever so simply.

YOU WILL NEED

- Plain tea towel, cotton
- Fabric block printing ink
- Ink tray
- Roller
- Sponges
- Paintbrush
- Fallen leaves
- Tape

Tip: This would look great as a border design printed along one edge of a piece of fabric, too.

TEA TOWEL

This is a wonderful no-sew project for a complete beginner. Use natural found objects, such as leaves, and turn them into stencils to create a beautiful printed tea towel. I've used my leaves to print a ready-made tea towel for a speedy handmade housewarming gift, as a home can never have too many tea towels!

01 Print your cotton tea towel using the Fallen Leaf Printing technique, just making sure that the hanging loop usually found on tea towels is at the top before you begin.

02 Dry and fix the print following the instructions on your printing inks. I use a hairdryer for speed then iron on the reverse to heat set the ink.

03 Your ready-made tea towel has already been hemmed for you, but if not just hem (see Sewing Techniques) all four edges then hang it up for all to see!

YOU WILL NEED

- Printed tea towel, approx 45 x 75cm (17¾ x 29½in)
- Hairdryer
- Iron

Tip: This is such a versatile technique – you can use it to make a table runner, napkins and placemats with single or multiple leaf prints.

PAINTBRUSH PRINTING

The simplest of tools can create the most beautiful of prints. There is something lovely about the marks you can make with just a paintbrush and some ink. This technique for fabric printing focuses on the simplicity of the idea of mark making in print design and is a truly valuable skill.

01 Carefully select the paintbrushes you will be using for this project. I chose three different sized ones with soft textures, as I want to see the fibres when printing. Put your ink on a plate

02 Using a piece of scrap fabric, experiment with the marks you can make with your chosen brushes and fabric ink. Vary the pressure and stroke widths to create interesting marks then select your favourite ready for printing.

03 Set up your printing fabric, pressing it to remove any visible creases before taping it into place. Mark in pencil or trick marker a guideline for your repeat pattern design – I set the elements of my design about 5cm (2in) apart.

04 Start painting the ink onto the fabric as marked. On the plate, adjust the consistency of the ink as necessary with a little water – I find the technique works best when the ink is quite thick.

05 Build up your print design with your chosen brush marks, following the guidelines you have marked.

YOU WILL NEED

- Fabric, medium to heavyweight
- Fabric screen printing ink
- Paintbrushes, wide width
- Plate for ink
- Trick marker or pencil
- Scissors
- Ruler
- Tape
- Iron
- Scrap fabric

Tip: Mix and match the brush strokes and marks that you make to create a more irregular and interesting print design.

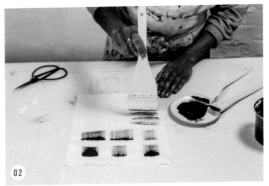

BEANBAG

This beanbag printed with a brush mark design is the perfect addition to any living space or playroom – I've kept it classic and monochrome to fit in with any interior. Advance your sewing skills with this larger scale project – if you enjoyed crafting the pyramid doorstop, this is the larger version!

01 Draw and cut out your fabric pieces for each section of the beanbag, following the dimensions given (A). Print using the Paintbrush Printing technique then dry and fix your fabric according to the instructions on your fabric printing inks.

02 Place two of the four printed main body pieces right sides together and pin. Sew along the right-hand side with a 1.5cm (⅝in) seam allowance then finish the seams (see Sewing Techniques) (B). Repeat for the other two sides of fabric.

03 Now place the two panels together with the right sides facing, pin into place and stitch along the seams. Then press and finish the seams – you should now have a completed middle section of the beanbag with the right sides facing inwards (C).

04 With the right side of the top panel facing up, align the handle edges centrally with the panel's raw sides and pin it. With a 1cm (½in) seam allowance, sew each end securely backwards and forwards to add extra strength, and reverse at the start and finish to really secure the stitching (D).

05 With the right sides facing, match the top panel's corners to the seams of the main body and ease it into place, aligning the raw edges and pinning when happy. Then slowly sew into place with a 1.5cm seam allowance. Repeat this process for the bottom panel, leaving a 25cm (10in) gap along one edge then reversing at the start and finish to secure.

06 Now turn the beanbag right side out, pulling the fabric carefully through the gap you left earlier. Press the seams then fill with beanbag filling, turning the raw edges inside before pinning and finishing by hand with a slip stitch (see Sewing Techniques).

YOU WILL NEED

- Four pieces of printed fabric for beanbag body, (see Step 01)
- Printed fabric for the top, 20 × 20cm (8 × 8in)
- Base felt fabric, 65 × 65cm (25½ × 25½in)
- Leather or similar for handle, 28 × 3cm (11 × 1¼in)
- Sewing machine and matching thread
- Hand-sewing needle
- Scissors
- Measuring tape
- Beanbag filling
- Iron

Tip: You could print and make a handle with a smaller scale version of the main body pattern, or use a fabric in a contrasting colour to personalize your beanbag.

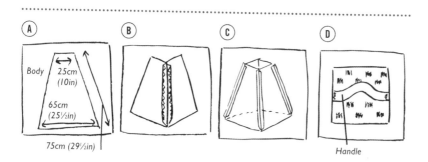

SCREEN PRINTING WITH MASKING TAPE

I wanted to share a quick and easy method of creating a stencil for silk screen printing using just a roll of masking tape. You can block out areas of your silk screen with low-tack tape of varying widths to create geometric, gridded and striped designs. The possibilities are endless, and so quick you'll have a bank of geometrical printed fabrics in no time at all!

01 Mark a grid pattern onto the plain paper by tracing around the Grid Envelope Cushion template (see Templates) nine times to create nine blocks evenly laid out within your paper square.

02 Turn your screen so the mesh side is facing up, then position it above your grid template, so you can see the pencil lines clearly through the mesh. Using these as a guide, apply masking tape directly onto the screen mesh, following the pencil lines. Repeat for each line then mask all the way around the edge of the square, taking care not to leave any gaps in the mesh where ink could leak through.

03 Prepare your fabric for printing by making sure it is ironed and secured in place with masking tape – it is important that the fabric does not move during the printing process to prevent any blurred prints. Use the paper template to roughly mark the top and bottom of your design with a pencil, making sure it is centred on the fabric.

04 Line up the screen on the fabric as marked, mesh side down, making sure there is enough excess fabric at the top and bottom for your seam allowances and that it is evenly spaced.

05 Now you are ready to print. Spoon the ink along the top edge of your silk screen and spread this evenly. Holding the frame with one hand and the squeegee with the other, set the squeegee into the ink. Then hold at a 45-degree angle and press firmly while you pull the squeegee towards you with one continuous motion. Look through the screen mesh to make sure you have printed evenly then repeat this process once more.

06 Set your squeegee to one side on the piece of scrap paper. Carefully lift the screen from one side to the other to reveal your grid print and hang it up to dry. Wash out your screen with cold water immediately, then leave this to dry, too.

You Will Need

- Plain fabric, medium to heavyweight linen or cotton
- Fabric screen printing ink
- Silk screen
- Squeegee
- Spoon
- Pencil
- Scissors
- Masking tape
- Plain paper, 30 x 30cm (12 x 12in)
- Scrap paper

Tip: Create pattern variations by mixing different widths of masking tape to build your designs. Repeat the process to add another colour and bring your design some dimension.

GRID ENVELOPE CUSHION

If you've never made a cushion before, this is by far the easiest and quickest way to do so. By using one continuous length of fabric and folding the edges in towards themselves, you can create a simple envelope-back cushion cover. Experiment with shapes and colours to totally transform your sofa with cushions!

01 Measure 25cm (10in) in from each of the short edges of your fabric then create a line across the width with the trick marker – the area between these two lines will be your print area (A). Now print the grid design through the centre of your fabric using the Grid Envelope Cushion template and the Screen Printing with Masking Tape technique.

02 Dry and fix the fabric by referring to the instructions on your fabric ink. Using a sewing machine and matching thread, zigzag stitch (see Sewing Techniques) the raw edges on the shorter sides of the fabric to finish them.

03 With the right side of your fabric facing down, use your trick marker to mark a line 5cm (2in) in from each of these short finished edges. Fold and crease the fabric along these lines with an iron (B).

04 Using the edges of your printed design as a guide, fold the right and left edges into the centre and press them into place, laying one flat on top of the other (C).

05 With the trick marker, now draw a stitch line across the top and bottom edge of the fabric, again using the print line as a guide (D). Then pin the edges and centre in place with pins at right angles to the lines.

06 Stitch along the lines using your sewing machine or by hand using back stitch (see Sewing Techniques). Then use scissors to trim any excess fabric and clip the corners before turning the cushion cover the right side out. Press and fill this with a cushion inner.

YOU WILL NEED

- Printed fabric, 80 x 33cm ((31½ x 13in)
- Cushion inner, 30 x 30cm (12 x 12in)
- Sewing machine and matching thread
- Hand-sewing needle
- Trick marker
- Pencil
- Scissors
- Tape measure
- Pins
- Iron

Tip: Add buttonholes with your sewing machine then sew on some buttons as decorative closures for your cushion.

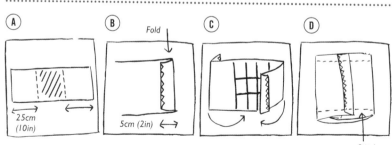

(A) 25cm (10in)

(B) Fold · 5cm (2in)

(C)

(D) Stitch

FOAM BRUSH PRINTING

The foam brush is another artist's tool – by applying a varied pressure it can be used to make wonderful printed textures and marks. Paint directly onto your fabric using these brushes to create stunning geometric pattern designs that have a truly handmade charm.

01 Mix up your chosen coloured inks in small quantities, diluting them by adding a little hot water at a time to achieve the desired colour intensity and testing them on some scrap fabric as you go.

02 Using a scrap piece of fabric, now test your foam brushes and experiment with the marks you can make with them. Dip the brushes directly into the ink and apply different levels of pressure to each, using the tip as well as the full head to build ideas for your print design.

03 Cut and press your fabric ready for printing. Then secure it into place with tape so it doesn't move while you are printing.

04 Having chosen the marks you will be using for your final design, carefully print your fabric. Use a pencil or trick marker to make a guideline for printing, if needed.

05 Repeat this process for all your fabric pieces.

YOU WILL NEED

- Fabric, medium to heavyweight
- Fabric dyes for hand use
- Water
- Foam brushes
- Tape
- Scrap fabric

Tip: When mixing up your inks, add a very little amount of water at a time – if they are too runny they may bleed into the fabric.

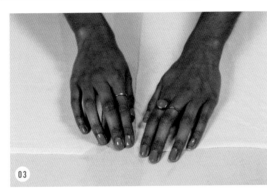

PATCHWORK BOLSTER

Bolsters really complement a collection of cushions – you can add one to your bed, which will be perfect for propping yourself up on while you are reading. When you sew up this bolster you'll be able to practise a simple method for patchwork and develop your sewing skills, too.

01 Print your fabric pieces using the Foam Brush Printing technique then leave to dry naturally or blow-dry with a hairdryer. Fix your design before pressing the fabric flat, ready for sewing.

02 Join together the three fabric pieces that will form the body of your bolster pillow. Place pieces A and B together, right sides facing, then use your sewing machine to stitch with a 1.5cm (⅝in) seam allowance along the right-hand side of the fabric. Repeat this process for pieces B and C, so you end up with one wide piece of fabric (A). If you don't have a sewing machine, you can sew them by hand with a close running stitch or back stitch (see Sewing Techniques) instead.

03 Press the seams open, then trim and zigzag stitch (see Sewing Techniques) the edges to prevent any fraying. It is important to keep the seams neat and tidy when building any type of patchwork.

04 With the right sides facing, join together the two long edges. You should now have a hollow tube with the right sides facing each other (B).

05 Attach one end panel by first using scissors to snip small notches (see Sewing Techniques) around the edge of one plain fabric disc. With the right sides facing, ease it into the hole at one end and pin into place (C). Using either your sewing machine, or a close running stitch or back stitch (see Sewing Techniques), sew this carefully and slowly into place, leaving a 1.5cm (⅝in) seam allowance. Repeat for the other end piece but only sew half way.

06 Turn the bolster cover the right side out by pulling the fabric through the gap in one end. Press the seams to finish then fill with the inner. Tuck the raw edges inside and pin into place then sew them together using a slip stitch (see Sewing Techniques). Your patchwork bolster is now complete!

YOU WILL NEED

- Three pieces of printed fabric, 58 × 18cm (23 × 7in)
- Two discs of plain fabric, 20cm (8in) in diameter
- Bolster cushion inner, 45 × 17cm (17¾ × 6¾in)
- Sewing machine and matching thread
- Hand-sewing needle
- Scissors
- Tape measure
- Pins
- Hairdryer
- Iron

Tip: When you ease the end panels into the main body of the bolster fabric, take your time – you can add the odd crease here and there to help with the fit. Make sure you cut your fabric and pattern as accurately as you can to ensure the perfect fit.

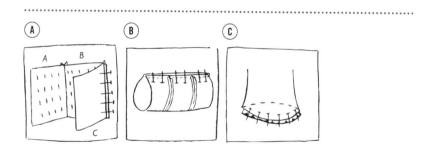

LINO BLOCK PRINTING

The lino block printing technique allows you to create a versatile and re-useable rubber stamp on which you can carve your own design. Print a repeat pattern or an all-over design by creating two or three different blocks. This technique works really well for simpler designs and fabric items that you want to personalize with one print rather than cover completely with a pattern, providing you with endless printing possibilities!

01 Using the tracing paper and soft leaded pencil, transfer trace the Leafy Shopping Bag template (see Templates) onto your lino block.

02 With the lino cutter, carve away any areas of the lino block that you do not want to print – only raised areas will become your print design, so you are removing the negative space or background. Do this by keeping your fingers behind the blade at all times, gradually gouging out small areas by gently pressing the cutter into the block. The key is to gouge away shallow pieces of lino slowly rather than to dig the blade into the block.

03 To check you have carved enough of the lino, test your print by dabbing the inkpad firmly onto the lino so the surface is evenly covered in ink. Then use one hand to firmly and evenly press the lino block face down onto your sheet of scrap paper, holding it in place with the other hand so it doesn't move. Lift up the block to reveal your print, so you can assess whether you need to carve your design any deeper.

04 Iron your fabric then position it on some scrap paper to avoid a mess. Squeeze a small amount of ink into your ink tray and roll it out as evenly and finely as you can. Then roll some ink onto your lino block, making sure it is evenly covered for the best print.

05 You are now ready to print. Flip the lino block and place it on your fabric face down, as carefully as you can. Hold it in place with one hand so it can't move and use a clean roller to gently roll on top of the lino block – this will add more pressure to create the perfect print. Lift up to reveal your print, then repeat this process for each colour and shape to build up your design.

YOU WILL NEED

- Plain fabric, medium to heavyweight
- Inkpads for stamps
- Opaque fabric block printing inks
- Ink tray
- Two rollers or brayers
- Lino block, speedy carve, soft cut or master cut
- Lino cutter
- Soft leaded pencil
- Iron
- Tracing paper
- Scrap paper

Tip: Try not to print too close to the edge of your fabric – always start from the centre and work out when creating a design to allow for your seams and to achieve the best layout.

01

02

03

04

05

LEAFY SHOPPING BAG

With its added gusset, this project is a great alternative to an everyday tote bag. It makes the perfect shopping bag and looks super-stylish!

01 Print your fabric using the Leafy Shopping Bag template and the Lino Block Printing technique. Dry and fix your fabric by following the instructions on your fabric ink – I use a hairdryer on the front and iron the reverse to speed up the drying process.

02 Place your two pieces of fabric with the right sides together, making sure the top edges are aligned (A). With a pencil or trick marker, mark a 1.5cm (⅝in) seam allowance around the sides and bottom of your bag and pin at right angles. Now sew the edges together, using a straight stitch and reversing at the top and bottom edges.

03 To create the gusset for the tote bag, mark a 6cm (2⅜in) square at both the bottom corners of your bag, then cut each square out (B). You will be cutting through your stitch line but don't worry, all will become clear!

04 At one corner, press the cut seams together so they form a diamond-shaped gap. Close the gap, aligning the cut stitch line at both sides, then flatten together and pin into place (C). Sew across the new seam with a 1.5cm (⅝in) seam allowance to create your gusset. Simple! Remove the pins and repeat for the other corner then finish the raw edges (see Sewing Techniques).

05 Turn the top edge of your bag 1.5cm (⅝in) under, press and repeat to create a nice edge along the top of your bag. Pin at right angles and sew in place as close to the fold as you can (D). Then turn the right side out, press once more and you are ready to attach your handles.

06 Cut two strips of leather, each measuring 75 x 3cm (29½ x 1⅛in), to create the shoulder straps. Mark a small cross in pencil where your straps will fix to each side of the bag, around 6cm (2⅜in) down from the top and 10cm (4in) in from the side seams. Stitch securely into place using a leather sewing needle on your machine.

YOU WILL NEED

- Two pieces of printed fabric, 45 x 40cm (17¾ x 15¾in)
- Two pieces of leather for straps, 75 x 3cm (29½ x 1⅛in)
- Sewing machine and matching thread
- Leather sewing machine needle
- Pencil or trick marker
- Scissors
- Ruler or tape measure
- Pins

Tip: You could use any material for your straps – go with a contrasting colour, faux leather, or a matching piece of cotton to really make it yours!

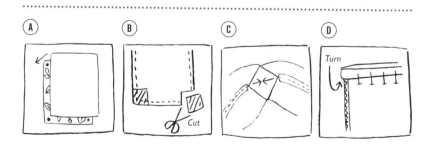

SCREEN PRINTING WITH FREEZER PAPER STENCILS

By using freezer paper to create stencils to print with on an open screen you can cleverly build up a multi-coloured fabric print from scratch with minimal equipment.

01 Cut two pieces of freezer paper with scissors to fit your silk screen. Trace one Fox Design template (see Templates) at the centre of each sheet and label with the corresponding letter. Using a scalpel and cutting mat, carefully cut out the coloured areas of your design, keeping any loose pieces that you cut out for later.

02 Iron your fabric, lay it flat and secure the edges with masking tape. Carefully lay stencil A directly onto the fabric, making sure the freezer paper has its waxy side facing down, then gently iron the stencil so it sticks to the fabric – don't over-iron, otherwise it will be difficult to peel away later. You can also place the floating pieces into position now and secure them by ironing.

03 To prepare your silk screen for printing, mask where the mesh meets the edge of the frame on the reverse or flat side of the screen with wide-width masking tape – this stops any ink spilling through the edges and bleeding onto your fabric.

04 Place your screen directly on top of your freezer paper stencil, checking you can see the entire design through the mesh, then dollop a generous line of ink evenly across the top edge of the screen. Holding your squeegee at a 45-degree angle in one hand, use the other to hold the frame securely. Press the squeegee down into the ink and pull it towards you in one continuous motion until you reach the bottom of the screen – then repeat the process in the opposite direction. Give the squeegee a bang to release any excess ink back onto the frame and repeat the process. Slowly lift up your silk screen from the end closest to you to reveal the print – the paper should remain stuck to the fabric. The ink will need to dry before moving onto colour B, so wash your silk screen and squeegee immediately with cold water and a sponge then leave them to dry naturally before printing again.

05 When your print is completely dry (you can use a hairdryer to speed this along!) peel away your paper stencil and iron your fabric again ready to repeat the whole process for your colour B stencil.

YOU WILL NEED

- Plain fabric, medium or heavyweight
- Two fabric screen printing inks, contrasting colours
- Silk screen
- Squeegee
- Sponge
- Freezer paper
- Pencil
- Scissors
- Scalpel and cutting mat
- Masking tape, wide width
- Iron
- Scrap paper, newspaper or table protector

Tip: As you grow in confidence, you can start to add multiple colours by simply using different layers of stencils, a process known as colour separation.

FOX-SHAPED PILLOW

This cute little fox-shaped pillow is the perfect creature to adorn you home, or why not give your fox to some friends? Bring him to life with a simple screen print and a bit of stitching – alternatively you can use this technique to create any shape of pillow you wish.

01 Print the Fox Design template onto your fabric using the Screen Printing with Freezer Paper Stencils technique. Then dry and fix by following the instructions on your ink.

02 Lay your printed and backing fabrics together, right sides facing (A). Measure a 1.5cm (⅝in) seam allowance in from the edge of the print and mark a stitch line all the way around your design.

03 Pin the fabrics together at right angles then use your sewing machine to stitch along your marked line, reversing at the beginning and end – you can sew this by hand with a close running stitch or back stitch (see Sewing Techniques) if you don't have a sewing machine (B). Remember to leave a 10cm (4in) gap for filling.

04 After you have stitched your fabrics together, trim away the excess material then use pinking shears or finish with a zigzag stitch (see Sewing Techniques) to prevent any fraying edges (C).

05 Snip notches (see Sewing Techniques) into any inward curves to enable the cushion to take its intended shape (D). Then turn it the right side out, making sure you poke out all the corners, perhaps using a blunt pencil or chopstick to help.

06 Press with your iron and fill your fox with toy stuffing or a scrap fabric. Pin the gap closed and slip stitch (see Sewing Techniques) with a needle and thread. Finished!

YOU WILL NEED

- Printed fabric, 30 × 25cm (12 × 10in)
- Plain or patterned fabric, 30 × 25cm (12 × 10in)
- Sewing machine and matching thread
- Hand-sewing needle
- Scissors
- Pinking shears
- Pins
- Toy stuffing or scrap fabric for filling
- Iron

Tip: If you don't have any toy stuffing or scrap fabric you're willing to part with, old tights make great alternative fillers!

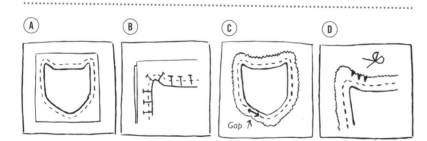

STENCIL PRINTING WITH TORN PAPER TAPE

I love paper tape and have a seemingly endless collection... it's great for gift-wrapping and decorative projects, but you can also use it to make stencils for fabric printing. By tearing off pieces of the tape and sticking them to your fabric you can use the tape to block ink and create a negative print for a completely one-off design.

01 Cut your fabric into rectangles and mark out the print area within each by using the trick marker to draw a line for the seam allowance all the way around. Then use the ruler to mark a point every 2 to 3cm (¾ to 1⅛in) in all directions, which is where you will fix your tape pieces.

02 Tear off small sections of the paper tape that are approximately 1cm (½in) wide – the rough edges will add to the design – then stick these directly on the fabric on the points you marked in Step 1.

03 Position your fabric on some scrap paper, taping it into place to prevent it moving while you are printing. Prepare your ink, dollop a spoonful into your ink tray and use your sponge roller to roll it out evenly.

04 Now roll the inked-up sponge roller directly onto your fabric, adjusting the pressure to create the desired print effect. I like the uneven quality this technique produces, so I roll the roller backwards and forwards a few times to build up the colour while maintaining a speckled look.

05 Leave your fabric to dry, or dry it with a hairdryer. Then peel away the pieces of tape to reveal your finished printed design.

YOU WILL NEED

- Plain fabric, medium weight
- Fabric block printing ink
- Ink tray
- Plastic spoon
- Sponge roller
- Paper tape
- Trick marker
- Ruler
- Hairdryer
- Scrap paper

Tip: Slightly angle your pieces of tape when you stick them to the fabric so you create a more random and less rigid all-over print design.

01

02

03

04

05

ZIP POUCH

I always carry a zip pouch in my handbag filled with pocket change, make-up and all my odds and ends – these pouches are very handy for keeping the contents of your handbag organized. This is a great sewing project to ease you into the process of inserting a zip, and an easy one to customize. Make these pouches in a variety of shapes and sizes, so you'll soon have a pouch for everything!

01 Print both sides of your outer pouch fabric pieces using the Stencil Printing with Torn Paper Tape technique. Leave to dry then fix using the instructions on your printing inks.

02 Place together one piece of outer pouch fabric and one piece of lining fabric, wrong sides facing. With your zip open halfway and the right side up, pin one edge at right angles in line with the top edge of your fabric pieces – the right sides of the fabric and zip should be facing, with the teeth pointing away from the edge (A).

03 Using the zipper foot on your sewing machine, now sew as closely as you can along the teeth of your zipper, reversing at the start and finish. Just move the pull tab out of the way as you are sewing – by holding everything in place with your needle you will then be able to sew past it smoothly.

04 Repeat this process for the other side of the zip, lining up your fabric and zip so they cleanly match. Finish any raw edges with zigzag stitch (see Sewing Techniques) to prevent any fraying, then gently press the fabric flat, avoiding the teeth of the zip.

05 With the zip open halfway, fold the right sides of your pouch together and pin at right angles around the three open edges (B).

06 Stitch around all three edges of the pouch, leaving a 1cm (½in) seam allowance. Trim away any excess fabric and cut the corners before finishing the raw edges with a zigzag stitch (see Sewing Techniques) (C). Turn your pouch the right side out and press once more to finish, then fill it up and pop it in your handbag!

YOU WILL NEED

- Two pieces of printed fabric, 23 × 16cm (9 × 6¼in)
- Two pieces of lining fabric, 23 × 16cm (9 × 6¼in)
- Zip, 20cm (8in) in length
- Sewing machine with zipper foot and matching thread
- Scissors
- Tape measure
- Pins
- Iron

Tip: Before sewing the pouch together, top stitch (see Sewing Techniques) along the right side of the fabric close to the zip for a professional finish – this also helps any excess fabric inside from becoming caught in the teeth of the zip.

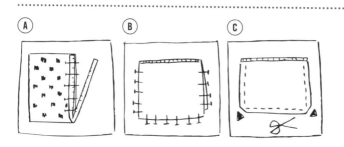

CARDBOARD TUBE PRINTING

There are so many ways to create a print design, especially by using the things you find in your recycling box at home. Old cardboard tubes lend themselves to printing perfectly, so this is a simple technique that you can easily replicate with any cardboard object to create a repeat pattern design.

01 Roll out a thin layer of ink into your ink tray. Spread it out as evenly and as finely as you can by repeatedly rolling it back and forth -- this will ensure the best results when you are printing.

02 Press the end of your cardboard tube firmly into the ink, making sure it is well coated when you lift it up. If not, press down once more and repeat until you can see the ink covering it evenly.

03 Use the ink-coated tube to print by pressing it down firmly on a piece of scrap fabric. Experiment with the marks different tubes make – overlap or squeeze them slightly to create variations of their original shapes.

04 Press your fabric flat, then mark a guideline for printing with a ruler and trick marker. This will guide your mark making and bring structure to your print design.

05 Print your fabric with your desired tube to create your pattern design, following the guidelines marked earlier.

YOU WILL NEED

- Plain fabric, heavyweight
- Fabric block printing ink
- Ink tray
- Roller
- Cardboard tubes
- Trick marker
- Scrap fabric

Tip: Create a striped pattern using different coloured inks and different tube shapes and sizes.

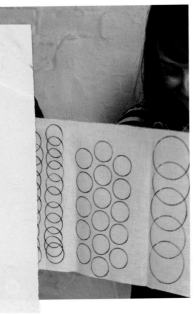

CIRCLES LAUNDRY BAG

Keep your dirty laundry in order with this structured storage bag. Its sturdy design and rope detailing has a certain nautical charm about it.

01 Cut out all your fabrics to the measurements provided. Print your design onto the body fabric using the Block Printing with Cardboard Tubes technique, then dry and fix ready to sew.

02 Fuse together the printed fabric and one piece of interfacing then the lining fabric and the other piece of interfacing with your iron.

03 With the wrong sides facing, lay out the printed fabric and lining fabric. Now pin them together along the short edges, right sides facing, and sew with a 1.5cm (⅝in) seam allowance to create a hollow tube of fabric layers (A).

04 With the right sides facing, attach the base fabric disc to the main bag shape. Fix in place with pins inserted at right angles all the way around, then carefully sew (B). Snip notches (see Sewing Techniques) in the fabric to help ease the disc into place. Finish the seams (see Sewing Techniques), then turn right side out.

05 Next make the channel for the rope to sit inside. With the wrong side face up, fold in the long edges on both sides of the channel fabric by 1cm (½in) and press into place (C). With the right sides facing, press the short edges of the channel together, then stitch them into one long loop with a 1.5cm (⅝in) seam allowance. Fold the entire piece in half lengthways and press again to hold in place.

06 Place the channel over the top of the raw edges of the bucket shape to hide them inside, and pin into place as evenly as you can the whole way around. Use your sewing machine to top stitch (see Sewing Techniques) into place as close to the fold as you can, leaving a 1.5cm (⅝in) seam allowance.

07 Carefully snip two slits on one side at the centre of the channel then thread your rope handles through. Knot to secure the ends, then move the knot through to the inside of the channel so it isn't visible to complete your laundry bag.

YOU WILL NEED

- Printed fabric for bag body, 110 × 30cm (44 × 12in)
- Lining fabric, 110 × 30cm (44 × 12in)
- Disc of base felt fabric, 35cm (13¾in) in diameter, 3mm (⅛in) thick
- Plain fabric for channel, 110 × 15cm (44 × 6in)
- Two pieces of firm weight iron-on interfacing, 110 × 30cm (44 × 12in)
- Rope, 1.25m (50in) in length
- Sewing machine and matching thread
- Scissors
- Iron

Tip: Finish your inside seams with bias binding for a neater finish.

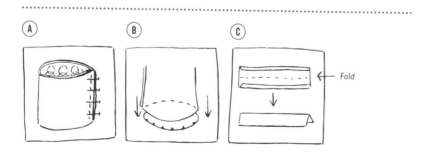

♥♥♥

STENCIL PRINTING WITH CUT TRACING PAPER

This is a wonderful project for personalizing items – a number, an initial, or even a name can be printed very simply onto fabric using this cut stencil technique. In fact, you will be monogramming everything in no time at all!

01 Trace the Number templates (see Templates) onto tracing paper with a pencil.

02 Then carefully cut out the shapes using a scalpel and cutting mat – you need to remove the positive space in this project.

03 Lay out your fabric so it is flat and press to remove any creases. Place the tracing paper stencil on top in the bottom right-hand corner and secure it in place with some tape.

04 Spread some fabric ink into a dish and roll it out using your soft sponge roller. Now evenly roll directly over your stencil and onto the fabric to create your print. Repeat this process for each stencil, experimenting with the pressure you put on the roller – I love the delicate marks created with a very light touch.

05 Use a different roller for each ink colour and repeat until you have printed all your stencils. Let the ink dry then peel the paper stencil away to reveal your print.

YOU WILL NEED

- Three pieces of fabric, medium to heavyweight
- Fabric block printing ink
- Ink tray
- Soft sponge rollers
- Pencil
- Scalpel and cutting mat
- Tape
- Tracing paper

Tip: Really personalize your prints by stencilling with names, initials or icons.

01

02

03

04

05

WALL TIDY

The English proverb 'A place for everything and everything in its place' couldn't be more fitting for this project. Keep your desk in order with this pocketed hanging organizer, which is just the place to store away all your stationery, and to keep magazines and newspapers tidy.

01 Print your fabric pockets using the Number templates and the Stencil Printing with Cut Tracing Paper technique. Dry and fix by following the instructions on your fabric inks – I use a hairdryer and iron to heat set.

02 With the wrong sides facing up, measure and turn under a 1.5cm (⅝in) seam allowance all the way around each pocket shape then press into place with an iron (A). Straight stitch along the top edge of each pocket 1cm (½in) in from the edge.

03 Using your ruler and trick marker, measure and mark where your pockets will fix to the backing fabric – I left a 10cm (4in) gap at the top and bottom of my backing then evenly spaced the pockets between. Pin the pockets into place then top stitch (see Sewing Techniques) around the sides and bottom of each, as close to the edges as you can (B).

04 Insert your rivets approximately 5cm (2in) from the top edge of your wall tidy, following the instructions that came with them – I placed one in the middle then evenly spaced the other two to the left and right (C). Hang the wall tidy up on your wall and fill it with all your stationery and magazines!

YOU WILL NEED

- Three printed fabric pockets, 35 x 25cm (13¾ x 10in)
- Plain felt fabric for backing, 90cm x 38cm (35½ x 15in), 3mm (⅛in) thick
- Sewing machine and matching thread
- Trick marker
- Tape measure
- Ruler
- Pins
- Three rivets
- Hairdryer
- Iron

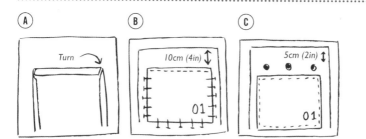

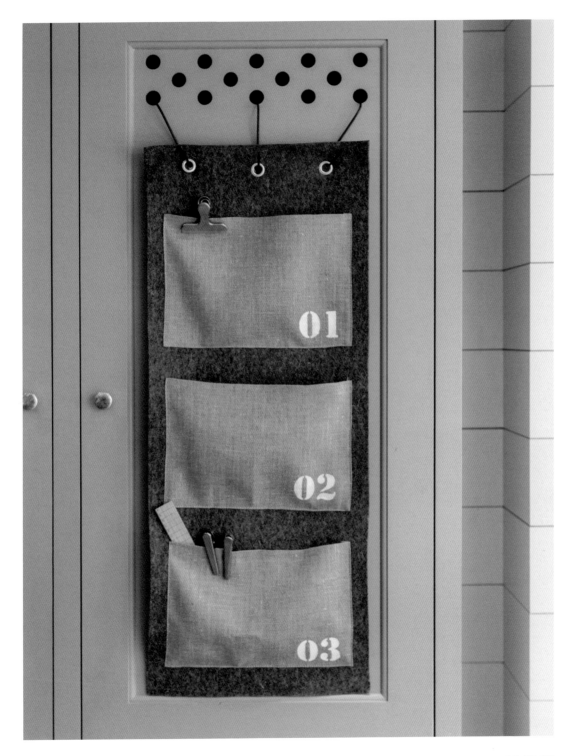

FRUIT AND VEGETABLE PRINTING

This technique is reminiscent of potato printing, which I used to do with my mum when I was a child – you can use the same process to print with almost any hard fruit or vegetable. Here I'll show you some tricks that use a cookie cutter, fruit and vegetables to create beautifully textured prints for your fabric projects in a very uncomplicated fashion.

01 This printing technique will work well with any hard fruit or vegetable. I've chosen apples, lemons and limes, celery, turnips, a swede and carrots for this project as they create really beautiful shapes when printed – celery can look like little semi circles, and apples can resemble hearts.

02 Carefully cut your selection of fruit and vegetables in half or into smaller sections, using a knife and chopping board.

03 Now use the cookie cutters to create symmetrical, more precise shapes from some of your vegetable sections. Slice a disc from your turnip then press your cookie cutter directly into the section to cut out your shape.

04 When you are happy with your selection of cut fruit and vegetables, test each piece on a scrap piece of fabric. Use a paintbrush to evenly apply fabric ink to each shape then press it down firmly onto the scrap fabric, lifting the shape up again to reveal your print.

05 Continue to experiment with the different shapes and sizes on your scrap fabric, and notice the lovely textures you can create using this technique. Have fun with repeat pattern ideas and enjoy the process.

06 Choose your favourite shape then print your fabric with a repeat pattern design. You can use a tape measure and trick marker to create a guideline to show where your repeat pattern should go.

YOU WILL NEED

- Fabric, light to medium weight
- Fabric block printing ink
- Ink tray
- Paintbrush
- Hard fruit and vegetables
- Knife and chopping board
- Cookie cutters
- Trick marker
- Scissors
- Tape measure
- Scrap fabric

Tip: There are no rules for print making – try building your print design organically by experimenting with scale and shapes to create a random pattern.

CIRCLE SKIRT

Having always enjoyed making my own clothing, I've fallen in love with dressmaking even more this past year. So I want to introduce it to you with this starter project, which is just right if you're a beginner. A circle skirt is very much how it sounds – made from a circular piece of fabric, it can be made to any length, a mini, midi or maxi. Add a waistband and a hem to your desired length, and you've made yourself a skirt!

01 Start with a square of fabric measuring no less than 1 x 1m (40 x 40in) – the exact size will depend on your waist measurements and the desired length. I chose my fabric to measure 115 x 115cm (46 x 46in), as I want my skirt to be a mini length.

02 With the right sides facing, fold your fabric in half, then in quarters.

03 To calculate the radius measurement for your waistline, measure your waist in centimetres then divide this measurement by 2 × Pi (3.14). For example, if my waist measures 75cm (29½in) and I divide this number by 2 × 3.14, the radius for the waistline of my skirt will be 12cm (4¾in) when rounded up.

04 Once you have calculated your own waistline radius, measure this distance from the centre corner of your folded fabric (the corner with no raw edges) and mark this at both edges of the fabric. Draw a curve between the points then cut out with scissors – you can attach a pencil to a piece of string to help you draw a smooth curve. Repeat this process for the skirt length measurement then cut away the excess fabric and unfold to reveal your disc-shaped circle skirt (A).

05 Print your disc-shaped fabric using the Fruit and Vegetable Printing technique. Dry and fix by following the instructions on your fabric inks then press to finish so you are ready to complete your skirt. I like to print my design once the skirt shape is cut to achieve the best layout for my repeat pattern.

YOU WILL NEED

- Printed fabric, as per your body measurements (see Step 01)
- Extra fabric for the waistband, your waist measurement plus a 1.5cm (⅝in) seam allowance at each end
- Zip, 15cm (6in) in length
- Sewing machine and matching thread
- Hand-sewing needle
- Trick marker
- Pencil
- Scissors
- Tape measure
- Pins
- Iron

(A)

Radius

Tip: Use a different print making technique to print a smaller scale pattern onto your waistband.

06 Cut a slit for your zip, which should be the same length as the zip you will be using.

07 Cut the fabric for your waistband so it is twice the desired finished width – I cut 15cm (6in) – and 3cm (1⅛in) longer than your waist measurement (see step 03).

08 Sew your waistband (see Sewing Techniques) then pin it to the top of your skirt, right sides facing, so the raw edges align. Sew the waistband and skirt together with a straight stitch, reversing at the start and finish to secure the seam. Then finish the seams off (see Sewing Techniques).

09 Insert the zip (see Sewing Techniques) and press. Then fold over the other side of the waistband and pin this into place, hiding the messy raw edges inside. Slip stitch (see Sewing Techniques) for a seamless finish then add a hook and eye at the top of your waistband for a professional touch.

10 Lastly, sew your hem with your sewing machine before pressing again to complete!

Tip: Try adding a border print or vary the scale to make more circle skirts.

WATERCOLOUR MARK PRINTING

I am always drawn to a striped design, whether it's coveting another stripy dress to add to my wardrobe or the design on a piece of fabric. Here is a very quick way to create your own set of stripes with some basic tools and fabric dyes. All you need is a paintbrush and a ruler then off you go...

01 Mix up your fabric dyes with a little water. Depending on how strong you would like the colour to be adjust the consistency little by little, testing where necessary on some scrap fabric. Avoid making your ink too watery to avoid unnecessary drip marks.

02 Using paintbrushes of different shapes and sizes, test the various stripe marks you can make on a scrap piece of fabric to build up a range of patterns.

03 Prepare your fabric for printing, pressing with an iron to remove any creases. Measure and mark the lines for your stripes on the fabric with the ruler and trick marker, making sure they are evenly spaced – I placed mine approximately 1cm (½in) apart.

04 Following your guidelines, paint your stripes onto the fabric with your chosen brush mark, alternating the start point from left to right.

05 Vary the brush marks to build a pattern within your stripe design, repeating this across the entire piece of fabric until complete. Leave to dry then fix following the instructions on your fabric dyes.

YOU WILL NEED

- Fabric, medium to heavyweight
- Fabric dyes for hand use
- Water
- Paintbrushes
- Trick marker
- Scissors
- Ruler
- Iron
- Scrap fabric

Tip: Spend some time experimenting with the amount of ink on your brush – I love the textures an almost dry brush can create.

LUNCH BAG

I'm determined to stop buying sandwiches for my lunch and to start making them instead, and this super-cute lunch bag is my material motivation! What nicer way to carry your lunch in to work than in one of these gusseted fabric lunch bags. Choose a sturdy and washable natural fabric to make this project for the best results.

01 Cut your fabric to size and print with the Watercolour and Brush Printing technique. Then dry and fix by following the instructions on your fabric dyes.

02 Cut and sew the loop (see Sewing Techniques) for your button closure with your sewing machine.

03 With the wrong side facing out, fold the printed fabric in half across the short edge to find the centre, then press to crease. Fold in 1cm (½in) from one of the short edges and press then fold over again to create a finished edge. Pin into place at right angles and stitch as closely to the fold as you can. Repeat for the other short edge, but this time slip the loop into the centre of the edge and pin into place. Press the loop away from the fabric so it is poking outwards, then stitch it into place as closely to the fold as you can, as before (A).

04 Now with the right sides together, fold your fabric in half so the short edges are aligned then press into place. Pin the long edges together and sew with a 1.5cm (⅝in) seam allowance (B). Finish the raw edges with bias binding or a zigzag stitch (see Sewing Techniques).

05 To create the gusset, still with wrong sides facing out, turn the bag so the side seams are in the centre and aligned. As you do this you'll be able to fold the diamond-shaped base towards the top of the bag – it should just fall into place (C). Press, then mark a 3cm (1¼in) line from each top and bottom corner with your pencil or trick marker and stitch across the lines. Trim and finish the raw edges with a zigzag stitch.

06 Turn the bag right side out then press the seams and gusset flat. Mark a point 14cm (5½in) from the button loop then sew your button securely here to complete your lunch bag.

YOU WILL NEED

- Printed fabric, 66 × 20cm (26 × 8in)
- Extra fabric for loop or ribbon, 8 × 3cm (3 × 1⅛in)
- Bias binding, 45cm (17¾in) in length
- Sewing machine and matching thread
- Pencil or trick marker
- Tape measure
- Pins
- Button
- Iron

Tip: Line your lunch bag with a waterproof fabric so it really is 'lunch proof' – this will mean you can easily wipe clean any spills and crumbs.

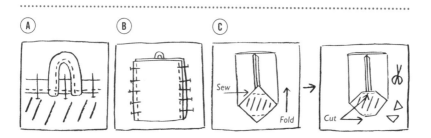

LINT ROLLER PRINTING

This is one of my favourite printing techniques – by using a lint roller as a rotary stamp tool you can create a perfectly printed piece of fabric in a flash. If you have children this is a great technique to work on together, as they'll have so much fun rolling their prints along the fabric!

01 Using the tracing paper and a soft leaded pencil, trace the Furoshiki Wrapping Cloth templates (see Templates) onto your foam sheet, then cut them out.

02 Experiment with the arrangement of foam shapes on your cutting mat. When you are happy, carefully peel away the backing of the lint roller to reveal the sticky side then place each shape onto the roller, pressing firmly into place.

03 Iron your fabric and place it on some scrap paper or a table protector, then fix it in place at the corners with a little masking tape. Prepare the ink by squeezing a small amount along the top edge of your ink tray.

04 Over-inking will produce a blotchy finish, so use a roller or brayer to roll the ink out in the tray as thinly as possible. The thinner the ink, the better the final print finish – you can always add more ink if you need it.

05 Gently drop your lint roller down into the top edge of the ink tray then carefully roll it towards you, making sure you press down firmly to cover every piece of foam.

06 Starting to work across the centre of your fabric, place your lint roller at one edge and very firmly roll it across the fabric width, stopping when you reach the other edge. Repeat this process above and below your first line of print to cover the entire piece of fabric with your design.

YOU WILL NEED

- Plain fabric, light or medium weight
- Opaque fabric block printing ink
- Ink tray
- Roller or brayer
- Lint roller
- A5 craft foam sheet
- Soft leaded pencil
- Scissors, or scalpel and cutting mat
- Masking tape
- Iron
- Tracing paper
- Scrap paper or table protector

Tip: This technique would work wonderfully as a border print design or across the centre of a table runner.

FUROSHIKI WRAPPING CLOTH

Furoshiki are ancient Japanese wrapping cloths that can be used to wrap an assortment of objects. I like to use them as an alternative to gift wrap – they make a lovely addition to any presents, and can then be used again and again.

01 Print your fabric using the Furoshiki Wrapping Cloth templates and the Lint Roller Printing technique. Dry and fix your fabric following the instructions given on your fabric ink – I use a hairdryer on the front to help speed up the drying process then iron the reverse to fix the ink.

02 Hem (see Sewing Techniques) around the edges of your wrapping cloth by folding 0.5cm (¼in) in on the wrong side of the fabric, pressing with an iron then folding over again.

03 Pin the fabric at right angles to keep it in place, fold your corners neatly underneath then use a sewing machine or a needle and thread to stitch as closely to the fold as you can.

04 Trim away any extra thread, remove the pins and press the hem to finish.

05 Follow the instructions shown in the diagram (A) to fold your beautiful furoshiki cloth and wrap a gift!

YOU WILL NEED

- Printed fabric, 42 × 42cm (16½ × 16½in)
- Sewing machine and matching thread
- Hand-sewing needle
- Pins
- Hairdryer
- Iron

Tip: If you're feeling confident with making this project, why not print both sides to create a lovely reversible wrapping cloth?

(A)

♥♡♡

STENCIL PRINTING WITH PAINTER'S TAPE

Painter's tape is a brilliant alternative to masking tape for stencil making. This low-tack tape works in a similar way, but unlike masking tape it doesn't allow any ink to bleed underneath its edges. This tape is perfect for this project where I'll be showing you how to create a more precise stencil that will look its best with a crisp print line.

01 Carefully cut the Painter's Tape templates (see Templates) out from your sheet of paper, using your scalpel and cutting mat.

02 Now tear off a section of painter's tape that is approximately 4 to 5cm (1½ to 2in) in length. Position a template in the centre of the tape, then use a pencil to trace around it.

03 Cut the shape out from the tape using your scalpel – you need to remove the positive space in this project while keeping the tape intact. Repeat this process with the various templates until you have enough tape pieces to cover your fabric.

04 Use the trick marker to mark a seam allowance onto your piece of fabric, as well as a rough guideline for your tape stencils. I marked mine unevenly to create a loose repeat print design.

05 Carefully unpeel the tape sections from your cutting mat so they don't tear then stick them into place on your fabric, following the guidelines you marked earlier. Make sure they are flat with no gaps.

06 When you are happy with the layout, dab the stencil brush into the ink then onto your stencil a few times to evenly cover the fabric. You will be able to see whether this is the case immediately, then add more or less ink as necessary.

07 Leave to dry naturally or dry with a hairdryer before peeling off the tape to reveal your print design.

YOU WILL NEED

- Plain fabric, lightweight
- Fabric block printing ink
- Dish
- Stencil brush
- Painter's tape, wide width
- Trick marker
- Pencil
- Scissors
- Scalpel and cutting mat
- Ruler
- Hairdryer

Tip: Work with a light layer of ink then build this up to create a denser colour to help achieve a crisp print finish.

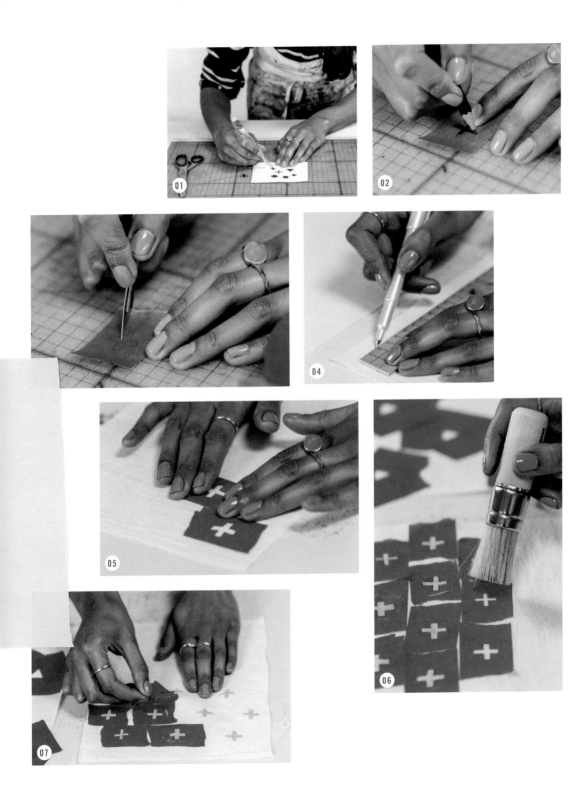

DRAWSTRING TRAVEL POUCHES

This is the ideal project for you if you're a beginner at sewing – simple drawstring pouches are effortless and fun to make. I use these for keeping things organized in my suitcase when travelling – I have one for jewellery, one for shoes, and one for my sketchbook and drawing pens. You can easily customize this pattern by adjusting the sizes to create an array of pouches for items large and small.

01 Print your fabric rectangles using the Painter's Tape templates and the Stencil Printing with Painter's Tape technique. Dry and fix your prints.

02 To sew the channel for your drawstring along the top edges of your fabric pieces, first measure 5cm (2in) down from the top right edge on one piece and make a 1cm (½in) cut into the fabric to create a flap. Turn the flap in 5mm (³⁄₁₆in) and press, then turn again and press once more. Now pin the flap into place before sewing it with your sewing machine as closely to the edge as you can (A). Repeat on the opposite side, and then again on both sides of the other fabric piece.

03 Fold over the top edge by 1cm (½in) then fold again, lining the edge up with the cut marks. Press into place, pin then sew as close to the edge as you can, reversing at the start and finish to secure the stitching (B). Repeat this process on the other fabric piece.

04 With right sides facing, place both pieces of fabric together, pin into place, then sew around the raw edges at the sides and bottom, leaving a 1.5cm (⅝in) seam allowance. Trim any excess fabric away using pinking shears, or zigzag stitch (see Sewing Techniques) the edges to finish.

05 Turn the pouch the right side out and press the seams. Cut the cord in half, then use a large safety pin to thread one half through the pouch channel from one side to the other. Repeat for the second piece of cord, but this time thread it through the opposite way. Pull through and knot each end.

YOU WILL NEED

- Two pieces of printed fabric, 25 × 18cm (10 × 7in)
- Cord, 72cm (28¾in)
- Sewing machine and matching thread
- Pencil
- Scissors
- Pinking shears
- Tape measure
- Pins
- Large safety pin
- Iron

Tip: Ribbon, cord or lacing works well as drawstrings for these little pouches – try a contrasting colour or pick a colour to match your print design.

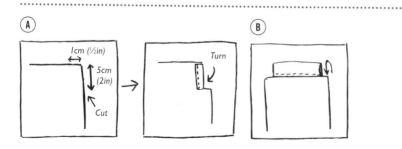

SCREEN PRINTING WITH AN EMBROIDERY HOOP

Advancing on from using masking tape and freezer paper stencils for screen printing, this is a clever way of creating a more detailed stencil for printing, while still using basic and inexpensive craft supplies. By using an embroidery hoop, organza and Mod Podge, you'll be able to paint a stencil ready to print repeat patterns onto fabric.

01 Stretch a piece of organza or muslin across your embroidery hoop, making sure it is taut with no creases. Tighten the screw on the hoop to secure into place, then trim off any excess fabric from around the edge using scissors.

02 Place the embroidery hoop fabric side down on top of your Infinity Scarf template (see Templates) and use a soft leaded pencil to trace the design directly onto the fabric.

03 Turning the embroidery hoop fabric side up, use a paintbrush to paint around your pencil marks with Mod Podge – you need to block out the negative space. Make sure you apply this in a smooth and even layer, leaving the shapes clear of any glue. Then leave to dry naturally for a few hours.

04 Prepre your fabric for printing by pressing it to remove any visible creases and taping it into place so it doesn't move during the printing process. Use your embroidery hoop and trick marker to mark where you will need to print each repeat of your design – it is always good practice to plan this in advance to achieve a precise pattern repeat.

05 Position your embroidery hoop onto the fabric then place a spoonful of ink at the top of the mesh. Using an old credit card as a squeegee, pull the ink firmly through the mesh towards you. Repeat backwards and forwards until the shapes are evenly coated.

06 Lift up the hoop to reveal your print then move it along to your next marker point and continue printing until you have covered your entire piece of fabric with your repeat pattern design.

YOU WILL NEED

- Fabric, lightweight, soft cotton
- Organza or muslin for mesh
- Fabric screen printing ink
- Embroidery hoop
- Old credit card or similar
- Plastic spoon
- Paintbrush
- Mod Podge
- Trick marker
- Soft leaded pencil
- Scissors
- Ruler
- Tape

Tip: Prepare your embroidery hoop screens in advance so you don't have to wait for your Mod Podge to dry. You can create multiple coloured designs by adding a different piece of organza for each layer.

01

02

03

04

05

06

INFINITY SCARF

Sew yourself the perfect printed fashion accessory – an infinity scarf. This is a simple sewing project that will have you making these for all your friends and family in no time at all. Try choosing a brightly coloured fabric for a super-chic scarf.

01 Print your fabric using the Infinity Scarf template and the Screen Printing with an Embroidery Hoop technique. Dry and fix your fabric following the instructions on your printing ink.

02 With the right sides facing, fold your fabric in half lengthways. Then pin and sew into place, leaving a 1.5cm (⅝in) seam allowance (A). Trim the excess, press the seams open with an iron and finish (see Sewing Techniques). You should now have a tube of fabric that is inside out.

03 To join the two open ends together, lay them flat on top of one other so the seams align. Starting from the seams, pin the edges together with the right sides facing, working around the width of the fabric opening to join the two sides to each other (B). Take your time, as this may be fiddly.

04 Sew together around the edges with a 1.5cm (⅝in) seam allowance – as you reach halfway you will need to readjust your fabric by turning it inside out, pulling it through the unsewn gap, to continue stitching the raw edges together. Leave a 10cm (4in) gap at the end, reversing to secure the stitching at both the start and finish.

05 Pull the right side of the scarf fabric through the gap then turn the raw edges inside and press. Sew the gap closed with slip stitch (see Sewing Techniques) to finish, then wear your scarf with pride!

YOU WILL NEED

- Printed fabric, 180 x 55cm (71½ x 22cm)
- Sewing machine and matching thread
- Hand-sewing needle
- Tape measure
- Pins
- Iron

Tip: Once you've mastered this technique you'll be whizzing up infinity scarves in no time. For a challenge, try making a patchwork version like the bolster cushion with three different pieces of printed fabrics.

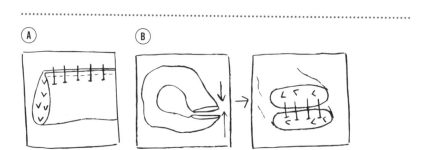

SCREEN PRINTING WITH PHOTO EMULSION

This is a more advanced method of screen printing and very exciting.
You can create a permanent stencil using a light sensitive photo
emulsion, which is perfect for repeat pattern printing projects
or longer one-off print runs. Although time-consuming, this
method allows you to achieve a much finer range of detail than
you would using any of the other stencil making processes.

01 Using the Lampshade Forest template provided (see Templates) prepare your artwork on acetate, either by tracing the design using a black permanent marker or by painting it on with a paintbrush and Indian ink, making sure the design is completely opaque.

02 Follow the instructions in your photo emulsion screen printing kit to coat the silk screen and set up your space for exposing the screen prior to printing. I use a lamp, black paper and plexiglass for this.

03 When the space is ready, remove your screen from the darkened area and tape the artwork to the back of the mesh, using some magic tape to secure it in place. Expose your screen and wash it out as described in your kit instructions – the image should now be permanently burnt onto your screen. Leave it to dry naturally, or dry it carefully with a hairdryer.

04 Prepare your fabric for printing, then tape it into place so it doesn't move. With your acetate stencil and screen, use masking tape or your trick marker to mark where the pattern repeats and therefore where you will need to place your screen each time you print to create a continuous pattern.

05 Cover any gaps between the edge of the silk screen frame and the underside of the mesh with masking tape to avoid any leaks before laying the screen onto the fabric ready to print. Then spoon your ink along the top edge of the silk screen, spreading it evenly from one side to the other.

06 Set the squeegee into the ink at a 45-degree angle then press down firmly and pull towards you in one continuous motion to print the design. Repeat once more.

07 Lift up the screen to reveal your print, lightly cover with some scrap paper and move the frame to the next point of printing as marked earlier. Continue this method until the fabric length is covered with your design.

YOU WILL NEED

- Fabric, medium weight
- Fabric screen printing ink
- Photo emulsion screen printing kit
- Silk screen
- Spoon
- Squeegee
- Acetate sheet
- Black permanent marker, or paintbrush and Indian ink
- Magic tape
- Trick marker
- Masking tape
- Lamp
- Plexiglass
- Hairdryer
- Black paper
- Scrap paper

Tip: Print the panels alternately to avoid smudging the wet ink when creating this repeat pattern.

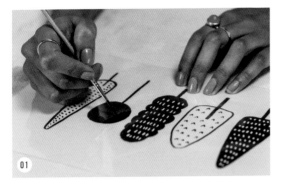

FOREST DRUM LAMPSHADE

Lampshades have always been one of those crafts that I thought would be too time-consuming or complicated to make at home – yet they are surprisingly straightforward once you know how. Craft your own professional repeat-printed drum lampshade in just one afternoon with a lampshade making kit – this is a much better alternative to buying one, and you'll be so proud of the results.

01 Print your fabric using the Lampshade Forest template and the Photo Emulsion Printing technique then dry and fix following the instructions on your printing ink. Iron your fabric as flat as you can, as it's important to remove any creases in the fabric before making your lampshade.

02 With your printed fabric facing the wrong side up, lay your laminate panel on top, making sure you are happy with the placement of the design. Ensure you keep the beginning of the print design well above the line of the kiss cut, as these will be snapped back later and could compromise your design if not allowed for. Then use a pencil to draw around the laminate, marking another guideline for a 1cm (½in) seam allowance all the way around too. Add an extra 1cm (½in) to the top and bottom of the left-hand side to create tabs that you'll need later to finish off the shade (A).

03 Keeping your laminate panel in place and using your pencil lines as guides, unpeel about 4cm (1½in) of the laminate and stick it directly onto your fabric as smoothly as you can (B). Make sure there are no creases in the fabric, but if you do find some just unpeel and re-stick until you are happy. Keep working all the way along the fabric until it has completely adhered to the laminate within the original guidelines.

YOU WILL NEED

- Drum lampshade making kit
- Printed fabric, size as per your kit
- Pencil
- Scissors
- Tape measure
- Iron

Tip: The more smoothly you apply the laminate to your fabric, the better the finish. Remove and reapply as many times as you need to until you are happy – and don't rush it!

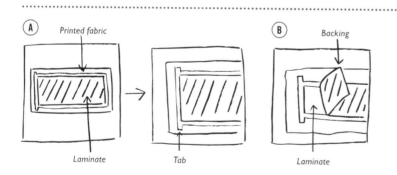

(A) Printed fabric

Laminate

Tab

(B) Backing

Laminate

04 Now trim away any excess fabric from around the laminate, right up to the edges, keeping the extra 1cm (½in) and tabs you marked in earlier. Snap back the kiss cuts on the laminate then carefully remove them (C).

05 Place a strip of double-sided tape along the left-hand side of the fabric strip and fold it over in towards the panel to create a tidy edge. Place another piece on the right-hand side of the fabric to stick in place later (D).

06 Smoothly cover the lampshade rings in double-sided tape then peel away the backing. I decided to make a table lampshade, so I placed the ring with the fitting at the bottom of my shade design –if you're making a ceiling pendant shade, place it at the top.

07 Starting from the left-hand side of the laminated fabric panel, position the edges of the rings at the top and bottom of where your fabric meets the panel then roll them forwards simultaneously. The key is to roll slowly and steadily until you reach the end of your fabric panel, keeping as close to the edge of the laminate as you can. The edges of the laminate panel and rings should align perfectly as you roll forwards.

08 When you reach the end, remove the backing from the piece of tape you applied in Step 5 and stick the edges together. You should now have a clean and tidy folded seam edge.

09 Using the plastic tool included in your kit, tuck the excess fabric over the edges and underneath the rings as tidily as you can (E).

10 Trim away any excess threads or fabric using scissors for a clean finish. Attach your lampshade to its base then stand back and admire!

Tip: You can use the rounded corner of a credit card to tuck the excess fabric underneath the lampshade rings for a lovely neat finish.

C

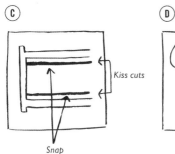

Kiss cuts

Snap

D

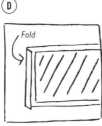

Fold

E

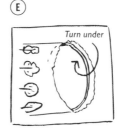

Turn under

STRING PRINTING

Wrap any household object with string to create a printing tool. This is a really fun technique that encourages you to experiment with mark making in order to develop a pattern design. I've used a glass bottle but you could use anything cylindrical – a rolling pin would work well, too.

01 Starting at the bottom of your cylindrical object, tape the end of the string in place. Then slowly unravel the string to wrap it around the object tightly so there is no slack.

02 Cross the string over in some areas and vary the spacing to create more interesting printing marks. When you reach the top, cut the string and tape this end to the underside of the bottle.

03 Roll out your fabric printing ink into the ink tray so it is evenly spread. Place the bottle into the ink and roll it repeatedly until all of the string is well coated with a layer of ink.

04 Starting at one side, place the bottle onto the fabric and roll it across to the other. Press down firmly to make sure all the ink transfers from the string to the fabric, creating an even print.

05 Build your design by rolling the bottle across the fabric from edge to edge. Change the starting point each time to create a varied print – I left a gap of a few centimetres between my prints to create a striped pattern. You can create a grid design very easily by rolling vertically at intervals across your fabric.

YOU WILL NEED

- Plain fabric, medium to heavyweight
- Fabric block printing ink
- Ink tray
- Roller
- Cylindrical object
- String
- Tape
- Scissors

Tip: Experiment on a piece of scrap fabric with different objects and arrangements of string for interesting pattern variations – there are endless possibilities with this type of printmaking.

01

02

04

05

PLANTER

Store your succulents in one of these lovely fabric planters. You can easily customize the size of your planter to any plant pot, add a handle then hang them up all over your home.

01 Print your fabric using the String Printing technique. Dry and fix by following the instructions on your fabric printing inks.

02 Use an iron to fuse an interfacing piece to the wrong side of the piece of lining fabric — they should match up exactly. Repeat for the printed piece of fabric, then the base piece.

03 With the right sides together, align the two short sides of the printed planter piece, pin them together and sew with a 1cm (½in) seam allowance, making sure you reverse at the start and finish to secure your seam (A). Press the seam open and finish the edges (see Sewing Techniques). Repeat for the lining piece to create two identical tubes.

04 With the right sides together, align the edges of the base fabric disc to the tube edges then carefully pin them into place (B). Cut notches (see Sewing Techniques) to help ease the curve into the tube then sew, leaving a 1cm (½in) seam allowance.

05 Turn out the printed tube of fabric and press. Fold 1cm (½in) from the top edge of each tube onto the wrong side of the fabrics and press into place for a tidy edge.

06 With the wrong sides facing, slip the lining fabric tube into the printed fabric tube. Line up the seams and make sure you push the two fabrics as closely together as you can (C).

07 Pin the top two fabric edges together, turning the raw edges inside evenly, and carefully stitch them into place as closely to the fold as you can to create a neat edge.

08 For a nice finishing touch, stitch a piece of leather at one side for a hanging strap. Fold over the top edge and pop in your plant!

YOU WILL NEED

- Printed fabric for planter sides, 53 × 17cm (21 × 6in)
- Lining fabric, size as above
- Two pieces of firm weight iron-on interfacing, sizes as above
- Two discs of base fabric, 16cm (6¼in) in diameter
- Two discs of firm weight interfacing, size as above
- Leather or similar for hanging strap
- Sewing machine and matching thread
- Trick marker
- Pencil
- Scissors
- Tape measure
- Ruler
- Pins
- Iron

Tip: Use a lining fabric in a darker contrasting colour to make the printed panel really stand out. This will also hide any plant residue!

SEWING TECHNIQUES

There are some basic sewing terminology and techniques used in the projects in this book, so I have compiled this section for you to use as a source of reference for your sewing.

RIGHT SIDE The printed side of your fabric, or top side.
WRONG SIDE The underside of your fabric, or reverse.

These are often abbreviated to RS and WS in sewing patterns.

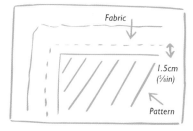

ADD A HEM First fold over a 1cm (½in) hem from the right side of your fabric. Press into place with an iron, then repeat so the raw edge is turned neatly underneath. Use your sewing machine and a simple running stitch to sew into place as close to the fold as you can. You can finish hems by hand with slip stitch, but this can be fairly time consuming.

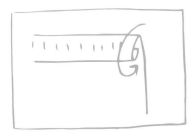

ADD A SEAM ALLOWANCE This simply means adding a 1.5cm (⅝in) allowance around every edge of fabric so that you do not lose valuable length for the seams within your sewing projects. It's good to bear this in mind when printing your fabric, so you don't cut off any vital parts of your print design.

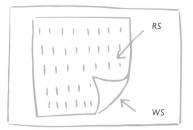

CUT NOTCHES Snip even sections or small triangles around any curves in your fabric to allow movement and to remove any awkward creases that might form. These are especially helpful when easing a curved piece of fabric into a straight edged piece of fabric.

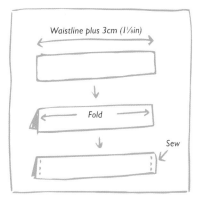

ADD A WAISTBAND To make a waistband, first measure your waistline, adding a 1.5cm (⅝in) seam allowance at each end. Cut out the fabric then fold this in half with the right sides facing. Stitch each end with a 1.5cm (⅝in) seam allowance then trim away the excess fabric. Now turn the fabric the right side out and press. Slip it over the top of your skirt, matching the seam to the opening of the waistband and, with the rights sides facing, use a simple running stitch on your sewing machine to sew one side into place. Fold over the other side, pin then neatly slip stitch this into place with a hand-sewing needle and matching thread to hide the raw edges inside.

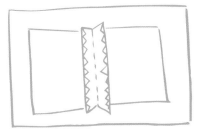

FINISH SEAMS To do this, press the seams open with an iron so they are flat. Trim the edges as neatly as you can to approximately 1cm (½in) then zigzag stitch, catching the edges of the fabric as you sew and reversing at the start and finish to secure the stitching. You can use an overlocker here if you have one, which will trim and sew the raw edges all in one go – or you can use a pair of pinking shears to trim the edges with a zigzag cut line to avoid fraying.

INSERT A ZIP Make sure your zip is open then line up one edge of the right side of your fabric with one edge of the right side of the zip and pin into place. Using the zipper foot on your sewing machine sew these together, reversing at the start and finish of the zip to firmly secure the stitching. Repeat this process for the other side. Remove the pins and do up your zip to make sure it is properly aligned.

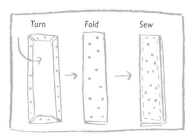

MAKE A LOOP OR HANDLE Towards the wrong side, turn down a 1cm (½in) seam allowance around each of the four edges of your fabric. Press into place then fold the whole piece in half with the wrong sides facing. Press and pin into place again then stitch as closely to the edge as you can, using a running stitch on your sewing machine. Use this technique to create any size of hanging or button loop, or a handle.

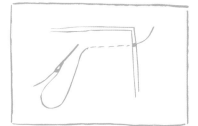

RUNNING STITCH This basic hand stitch can be used instead of a straight stitch on your sewing machine – just keep the stitches closely spaced for strength. Thread a hand-sewing needle, knot the end and pull it through your fabric from back to front until secure. Then insert your needle back through the front of the fabric a few millimetres along from where you began, pull tightly then continue, working back to front and front to back all the way along your seam.

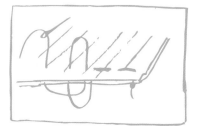

BACK STITCH A back stitch is a variation of the running stitch but smaller, stronger and slightly easier to keep straight, and it is another close alternative to machine stitching. Thread a hand-sewing needle with thread, knot the end and pull through from the back to the front until secure. Start with one stitch from the front to the back, then skip a stitch, pulling the needle back through after this skipped stitch. Push the needle back through the fabric in the opposite direction, working back towards your first stitch, then continue this way to complete your back stitch.

SLIP STITCH A slip stitch or invisible stitch is the perfect way to neatly close up any small seams in your sewing projects and can also be used for hemming by hand. Thread a hand-sewing needle and knot the end. Insert the needle into the underside of the seam then pull it through until the knot catches. Now insert your needle directly opposite the point you just came from and pull the thread taut. Repeat this process, pulling tightly, to close the seam invisibly. Knot the end and trim to finish.

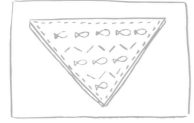

TOP STITCH Top stitching is an additional decorative line of stitching that is traditionally sewn very close to the edge of the fabric fold. Use your machine foot to ensure a measure of accuracy, but if you don't have a sewing machine you can do this with a hand-sewing needle and running stitch. You could also make top stitching into a decorative feature by choosing a contrasting colour and weight of thread.

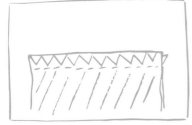

ZIGZAG STITCH This is also known as serging, and you can use this stitch to finish your raw edges if you don't have an overlocker. Using the zigzag stitch on your sewing machine, catch the raw edges of your fabric between the stitches to secure and stop fraying edges appearing in your projects.

TEMPLATES

In this section you will find all the templates you need for the projects in this book. Trace then cut them out following the instructions given in each project. Happy crafting!

100   150

HEXAGON TEMPLATE
Pencil End Printing project

BABY BIB TEMPLATES
Foam Stamp Printing project

INFINITY SCARF TEMPLATES
Screen Printing with an Embroidery Hoop project

GRID ENVELOPE CUSHION TEMPLATE

Screen Printing with Masking Tape project

LEAFY SHOPPING BAG TEMPLATES
Lino Block Printing project

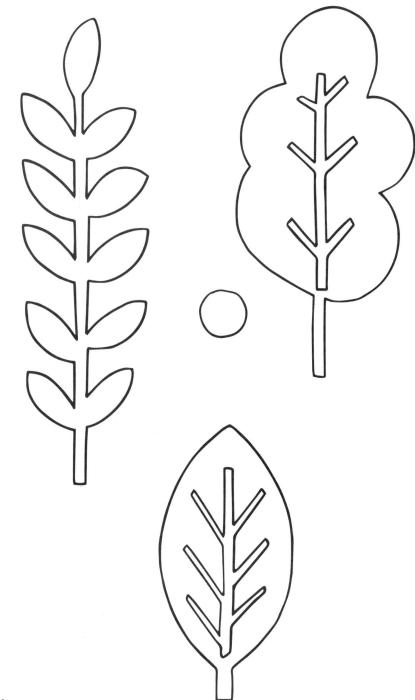

NUMBER TEMPLATES

Stencil Printing with Cut Tracing Paper project

(A)

PAINTER'S TAPE TEMPLATES
Stencil Printing with Paper Tape project

FUROSHIKI WRAPPING CLOTH TEMPLATES
Lint Roller Printing project

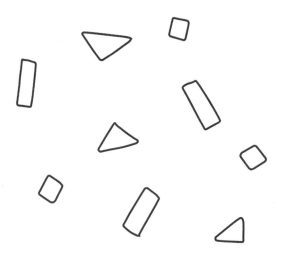

PYRAMID DOORSTOP TEMPLATES
Bleach Mark Printing project

PYRAMID DOORSTOP TEMPLATES
Bleach Mark Printing project

LAMPSHADE FOREST TEMPLATES
Screen Printing with Photo Emulsion project

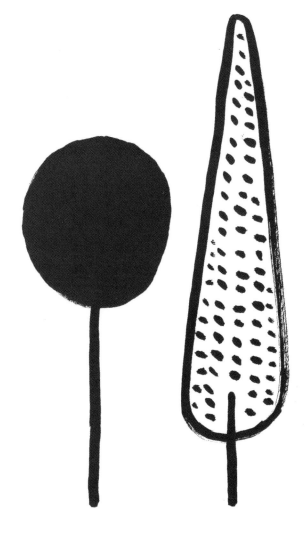

SUPPLIERS / RESOURCES

HANDPRINTED LTD

www.handprinted.net

Unit 6 Horton's Yard
Melbourne Road
Chichester
West Sussex PO19 7ND
Telephone 01243 697606

Everything you could possibly need for printing onto fabric in one place.

NEED CRAFT

www.needcraft.co.uk

13 Abbey Mead Industrial Park
Brooker Road
Waltham Abbey
Essex EN9 1HU
Telephone 01992 700311

Find a great selection of lampshade making kits and supplies here.

WICKED PRINTING STUFF

www.wickedprintingstuff.com

Unit 7 The Grove Workshops
Three Gales Road
Fawkham
Kent DA3 8NZ
Telephone 01474 709009

A more specialized supplier of screen printing supplies.

THE CLOTH HOUSE

www.theclothhouse.com

47 Berwick Street
London W1F 8SJ
Telephone 020 7437 5155

An inspiring emporium of beautiful and original fabrics that is definitely worth a visit for some samples.

THE CLEVER BAGGERS

www.thecleverbaggers.co.uk

Fox Buildings
Severn Road
Welshpool
Powys SY21 7AZ
Telephone 0845 2600 393

A great stockist of plain, printable tote bags and tea towels amongst other goodies.

BY HAND LONDON

www.byhandlondon.com

By Hand London is a brilliant place to start on your path to dressmaking. There are beginner patterns, sew-a-longs, plus an app to make a circle skirt!

ESSDEE

www.essdee.co

Educational Art & Craft
Supplies Limited
Edwin Avenue, Hoo Farm
Industrial Estate
Kidderminster
Worcestershire DY11 7SY
Telephone 01562 60787

The place to find all the tools you need for lino block printing and stamping.

WOOL FELT COMPANY

www.woolfeltcompany.co.uk

Unit 3 The Glade Business Centre
Forum Road
Nottingham NG5 9RW

A lovely selection of felt in different weights and colours.

CASS ART

www.cassart.co.uk

66-67 Colebrooke Row
London N1 8AB
Telephone 020 7354 2999

General art and craft supplies – you'll find a great selection of brushes here.

DALSTON MILL FABRICS

www.dalstonmillfabric.co.uk

69-73 Ridley Road
London E8 3NP
Telephone 020 7249 4129

A vast and inexpensive collection of fabrics – you'll find affordable cottons and linens here.

MACCULLOCH & WALLIS

www.macculloch.london

25-26 Dering Street
London W1S 1AT
Telephone 020 7629 0311

A great London haberdashery – find trimmings, cording, ribbons and bindings here.

RAY STITCH

raystitch.co.uk

99 Essex Road
London N1 2SJ
Telephone 020 7704 1060

A unique selection of fabrics and haberdashery too.

THE LAMPSHADE LOFT

www.thelampshadeloft.co.uk

Find a selection of gorgeous vintage and handmade lampshades here — they also run classes too.

EBAY

www.ebay.co.uk

I can always find everything I need here, no matter how obscure it is!

AMAZON

www.amazon.co.uk

Similar to eBay but ships to more countries worldwide — great for resource books and craft supplies.

ETSY

www.etsy.com

An online marketplace for hundreds of international crafters — find everything and anything here!

STITCH CRAFT CREATE

www.stitchcraftcreate.co.uk

A great online store for sewing materials, fabrics and other textile goods.

JOHN LEWIS

www.johnlewis.com

With stores all over the UK, this is great for haberdashery supplies, fabric and cushion inners.

MARTHA STEWART CRAFTS

www.marthastewart.com

Great for US readers, this store has everything you need for any craft.

PURL SOHO

www.purlsoho.com/purl

My favorite NYC sewing stop-off — a beautiful store filled with really unusual fabrics, which is great for sourcing plain neutral cottons and linens for printing.

TESSUTI

tessuti.com.au

This is a simply gorgeous fabric store that I visited in Sydney's Surry Hills. There is an online shop for all your fabric needs, and the store also runs sewing classes.

UTRECHTART

www.utrechtart.com

US based art supply store, which ships worldwide — great for tools, as well as general art and craft supplies.

ACKNOWLEDGMENTS

THANK YOU!

A huge thank you, firstly to Ame at FW for commissioning my first book and really making my dreams come true, to Ali for all her help and advice on the shoots, and to Emma for the answers to my many questions – I really couldn't have done it without all of your amazing support and patience. A special thank you also to lovely Freya for her wonderful and meticulous editing!

To Luke, Owen and Tori at Bread for the incredible work they did on this book, for understanding my vision, and for being the design and photography dream team that they are, as well as some of my best friends – thank you for being there along the way.

To my mum for teaching me how to craft! To Shef for always being on the end of the phone and for the last minute errand running! To Ellie for letting us use her beautiful flat for the location shoot – thank you. To Cathy, and to little Rafa for being my adorable baby bib model! To everyone at the studio, especially Becky, for all of their belief, encouragement and those late nights! To James for his gorgeous selection of props that I borrowed. And to everyone else for putting up with the chaos while writing this book.

Thank you to Stephen at Essdee, Shirley at Handprinted, and the team at Need Craft for their extremely generous and kind donation of supplies for the projects in this book. Also to the wonderful Jane Warren, thank you for teaching me how to make a lampshade.

Last but not least to my mum, dad, sisters and all my family and friends – thank you for your endless support, belief and encouragement, and foremost for putting up with me being a complete and utter workaholic all the time!!!

ABOUT THE AUTHOR

Zeena Shah is a London-based printed textile designer. She designs and crafts a collection of hand-screen printed goods for the home inspired by the everyday things she sees, as well as her love for Scandinavian and Japanese textiles. These handcrafted goods can be found in stockists both in the UK and internationally, and Zeena also creates print and pattern designs for individual clients and bespoke projects.

Zeena teaches silk screen printing workshops from her studio in East London, inspiring people to fall in love with printing and create something handmade. She also hosts pop-up workshops around London, spreading the printing bug as far as she can!

Find out more about her by visiting www.zeenashah.com

And you can view her visual diary at www.instagram.com/heartzeena

Share your creations by tagging #printwithzeena

♡ Zeena
X

INDEX

A DAVID & CHARLES BOOK

© F&W Media International, Ltd 2015

David & Charles is an imprint of F&W Media International, Ltd
Brunel House, Forde Close, Newton Abbot, TQ12 4PU, UK

F&W Media International, Ltd is a subsidiary of F+W Media, Inc
10151 Carver Road, Suite #200, Blue Ash, OH 45242, USA

Text and Designs © Zeena Shah 2015
Layout and Photography © F&W Media International, Ltd 2015

First published in the UK and USA in 2015

A catalogue record for this book is available from the British Library.

ISBN-13: 978-1-4463-0597-3 paperback
ISBN-10: 1-4463-0597-X paperback

ISBN-13: 978-1-4463-7261-6 PDF
ISBN-10: 1-4463-7261-8 PDF

ISBN-13: 978-1-4463-7460-9 EPUB
ISBN-10: 1-4463-7260-X EPUB

Printed in China by RR Donnelley for:
F&W Media International, Ltd
Brunel House, Forde Close, Newton Abbot, TQ12 4PU, UK

10 9 8 7 6 5 4 3 2 1

Acquisitions Editor: Ame Verso
Editorial Manager: Honor Head
Project Editors: Freya Dangerfield; Jane Trollope
Design: Bread Collective
Photography: Bread Collective
Art Direction: Ali Myer
Production Controller: Beverley Richardson

F+W Media publishes high quality books on a wide range of subjects.
For more great book ideas visit:
www.stitchcraftcreate.co.uk

Layout of the digital edition of this book may vary depending on reader hardware and display settings.

31901056531017